Marley

A Dog Like No Other

Also by
John Grogan

Marley & Me

Marley & Me Illustrated Edition

Bad Dog, Marley!

Marley
A Dog Like No Other

John Grogan

C Collins
An Imprint of HarperCollins*Publishers*

Library of Congress Cataloging-in-Publication
Data is available.

ISBN-10: 0-06-124033-8 (trade bdg.)
ISBN-13: 978-0-06-124033-1 (trade bdg.)
ISBN-10: 0-06-124034-6 (lib. bdg.)
ISBN-13: 978-0-06-124034-8 (lib. bdg.)

Typography by Sasha Illingworth
1 2 3 4 5 6 7 8 9 10

First Edition

To Ruth Howard Grogan,
who taught me the joy of a good story well told.

Contents

Preface
The Perfect Dog

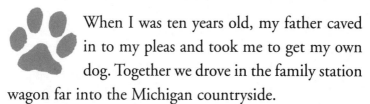When I was ten years old, my father caved in to my pleas and took me to get my own dog. Together we drove in the family station wagon far into the Michigan countryside.

We stopped at a farm run by a woman and her ancient mother. The farm didn't grow wheat or corn. It didn't even have cows or horses. It had just one thing—dogs. Dogs of every size and shape and age and temperament. They had only two things in common: Each was a mongrel, and each was free to a good home. We were at a mutt ranch.

"Now, take your time, son," Dad said. "Your decision today is going to be with you for many years to come."

I quickly decided the older dogs were not for me and raced to the puppy cage. "You want to pick one that's not timid," my father coached. "Try rattling the cage and see which ones aren't afraid."

I grabbed the chain-link gate and yanked on it with a loud clang. There were about a dozen puppies. They reeled backward, collapsing on top of one another in a squiggling heap of fur. Just one remained. He was gold with a white blaze on his chest, and he charged the gate, yapping fearlessly. He jumped up and excitedly licked my fingers through the fencing. It was love at first sight.

I brought him home in a cardboard box and named him Shaun. He was one of those dogs that give dogs a good name. He mastered every command I taught him and was naturally well behaved. I could drop a crust on the floor and he would not touch it until I said it was okay. When I called, he came. When I told him to stay, he stayed. We could let him out by himself at night, knowing he would be back after making his rounds. We could leave him alone in the house for hours, confident that he wouldn't have an accident or disturb a thing. He raced cars without chasing them and walked beside me without a leash. He could dive to the bottom of our lake and emerge with rocks so big they sometimes got stuck in his jaws. He loved riding in the car. He'd sit quietly in the backseat beside me on family road trips, happy to gaze out the window as the world zoomed by.

Best of all, I trained Shaun to pull me through the neighborhood dogsled-style as I sat on my bicycle. My friends jealously watched as he carefully guided me down the street, never leading me into trouble.

Shaun even had the good manners to back himself into the bushes before squatting to poop. With his rear end hidden away, only his head peered out. Our lawn was safe for bare feet.

Relatives would visit for the weekend and return home determined to buy a dog of their own. They were that impressed with Shaun. Actually, I called him "Saint Shaun." The saint part was a family joke, but we almost believed it.

Shaun had been born with a curse—no one knew who his parents were. Because his breeding was unknown, he was one of the tens of thousands of unwanted dogs in America. Yet by some stroke of good luck, he became wanted. He came into my life and I came into his. And he gave me the childhood every kid deserves.

Saint Shaun of my childhood. He was a perfect dog. At least that is how I will always remember him. It was Shaun who set the standard by which I would judge all other dogs to come.

1

And Puppy Makes Three

"Slow down, dingo, or you're going to miss it," Jenny scolded. "It should be coming up any second." Jenny was my wife. That January evening in 1991, we were driving through inky blackness across what had once been Florida swampland. We had been married for a little over a year and decided it was time for another family member. A dog, to be exact. We were on our way to look at a litter of Labrador retrievers.

Our headlights shined on a mailbox. The numbers

on the side reflected back at us. This was the place. I turned up a gravel drive that led into a large wooded property. There was a pond in front of the house and a small barn out back. At the door, a woman named Lori greeted us, with a big, calm yellow Labrador retriever by her side.

"This is Lily, the proud mama," Lori said. Lily's stomach was still swollen even though she'd given birth five weeks before.

Jenny and I got on our knees, and Lily happily accepted our affection. She was just what we pictured a Lab would be—sweet natured, affectionate, calm, and beautiful.

"Where's the father?" I asked.

"Oh," the woman said, hesitating for just a fraction of a second. "Sammy Boy? He's around here some-where." She quickly added, "I imagine you're dying to see the puppies."

Lori led us through the kitchen into a utility room. The puppies stumbled all over one another as they rushed to check out the strangers.

Jenny gasped. "I don't think I've ever seen anything so cute in my life," she said.

The litter consisted of five females and four males.

Lori was asking $400 for the females and $375 for the males. One of the males seemed particularly smitten with us. He was the goofiest of the group and charged into us. Somersaulting into our laps, he clawed his way up our shirts to lick our faces. He gnawed on our fingers with surprisingly sharp baby teeth and stomped clumsy circles around us on giant paws that were way too big for the rest of his body.

"That one there you can have for three hundred fifty dollars," Lori said.

"Aw, honey," Jenny cooed. "The little guy's on clearance!"

I had to admit he was pretty darn adorable. Frisky, too. Before I realized what he was up to, the rascal had chewed off half my watchband.

"We have to do the scare test," I said. I had told Jenny the story many times of picking out Saint Shaun when I was a boy. Sitting in this heap of pups, she rolled her eyes at me. "Seriously," I said. "It works."

I stood up and turned away from the puppies. Then I swung quickly back around, taking a sudden step toward them. I stomped my foot and barked out, "Hey!"

I didn't seem to scare any of them. But only one

plunged forward to meet the assault head-on. It was Clearance Dog. He plowed full steam into me, throwing a cross-body block across my ankles. Then he pounced at my shoelaces as though he was convinced they were dangerous enemies that needed to be destroyed.

"I think it's fate," Jenny said.

"Ya think?" I said. I scooped him up and held him in one hand in front of my face, studying his mug. He looked at me with heart-melting brown eyes and then nibbled my nose. I plopped him into Jenny's arms, where he did the same to her. "He certainly seems to like us," I said.

Clearance Dog was ours. We wrote Lori a check, and she told us we could return to take the dog home with us in three weeks, when he was eight weeks old. We thanked her, gave Lily one last pat, and said good-bye.

Walking to the car, I threw my arm around Jenny's shoulder and pulled her tight to me. "Can you believe it?" I said. "We actually got our dog!"

Just as we were reaching the car, we heard a commotion coming from the woods. Something was crashing through the brush—and breathing very heavily. It sounded like a creature from a horror film. And it was coming our way. We froze, staring into the darkness. The sound grew louder and closer. Then in a flash the thing burst into the clearing and came charging in our direction, a yellow blur. A very *big* yellow blur. As it galloped past, without stopping or noticing us, we could see it was a large Labrador retriever. But it was nothing like sweet Lily. This one was soaking wet and covered up to its belly in mud and burrs. Its tongue hung out wildly to one side. Froth flew off its jowls as it barreled past. I detected an odd, slightly crazed, yet somehow joyous gaze in its eyes. It was as though this animal had just seen a ghost—and couldn't possibly be more thrilled about it.

Then, with the roar of a stampeding herd of buffalo, it was gone, around the back of the house and out of sight. Jenny let out a little gasp.

"I think," I said, a slight queasiness rising in my gut, "we just met Dad."

2

Homeward Bound

When it was time to bring the dog home, Jenny was at Disney World with her sister's family, so I picked him up by myself.

Lori brought out my new dog from the back of the house. I gasped. The tiny, fuzzy puppy we had picked out three weeks earlier had more than doubled in size. He came barreling at me and ran head first into my ankles. He collapsed in a pile at my feet and rolled onto his back with his paws in the air. I hoped it was his way of telling me I was the boss.

Lori must have sensed my shock. "He's a growing boy, isn't he?" she said cheerily. "You should see him pack away the puppy chow!"

I leaned down and rubbed his belly. "Ready to go home, Marley?" I asked. That's what Jenny and I had decided to name him—after Bob Marley, our favorite reggae musician. It felt right.

I used beach towels to make a cozy nest for him on the passenger seat of the car. I set him down in it. But I was barely out of the driveway when he began squirming and wiggling his way out of the towels. He belly-crawled in my direction across the seat, whimpering.

At the center console, Marley ran into a problem. There he was, hind legs hanging over the passenger side of the console and front legs hanging over the driver's side. In the middle, his stomach was firmly beached on the emergency brake. His little legs were going in all directions, clawing at the air. He wiggled and rocked and swayed, but he was grounded like a freighter on a sandbar.

I reached over and ran my hand down his back. That made him squiggle even more. His hind paws desperately tried to dig into the carpeted hump between the two seats. Slowly he began working his hindquarters into the air, his butt rising up, up, until the law of gravity finally kicked in. He slid head first down the other side of the console, somersaulting onto the floor at my feet and flipping onto his back. From there he easily scrambled up into my lap.

Man, was he happy—desperately happy! He quaked with joy as he burrowed his head into my stomach and nibbled the buttons of my shirt. His tail slapped a steady beat on the steering wheel.

I found I could change the tempo of his wagging by touching him. When I had both hands on the wheel, his tail beat three thumps per second. *Thump. Thump. Thump.* If I pressed one finger against the top of his head, the rhythm jumped from a slow waltz to a lively bossa nova. *Thump-thump-thump-thump-thump-thump!* Two fingers and it jumped up to a mambo. *Thump-thumpa-thump-thump-thumpa-thump!* And when I cupped my entire hand over his head and massaged my fingers into his scalp, the beat exploded into a machine-gun, rapid-fire samba. *Thumpthump-thumpthumpthumpthumpthumpthump!*

"Wow! You've got rhythm!" I told him. "You really are a reggae dog."

When we got home, I led him inside and unhooked his leash. He began sniffing and didn't stop until he had sniffed every square inch of the place. Then he sat back and looked up at me with his head cocked as if he were saying, "Cool house, but where are my brothers and sisters?"

The reality of his new life didn't really hit him until bedtime. I had set up his sleeping quarters in the one-car garage attached to the side of the house. The room was dry and comfortable, and it had a rear door that led out into the fenced backyard. With its concrete floor and walls, it was virtually indestructible. "Marley," I said cheerfully, leading him out there, "this is your room."

I had scattered chew toys around, laid newspapers down in the middle of the floor, filled a bowl with water, and made a bed out of a cardboard box lined with an old bedspread.

"And here is where you'll be sleeping," I said, and lowered him into the box. He was used to sleeping in a box, but had always shared it with his siblings. Now he paced the perimeter of the box and sadly looked up at me. As a test, I stepped back into the house and closed the door. I stood and listened. At first nothing. Then a slight, barely audible whimper. And then full-fledged crying. It sounded like someone was in there torturing him.

I opened the door, and as soon as he saw me he stopped. I reached in and petted him for a couple of minutes. Then I left again. Standing on the other side of the door, I began to count. One, two, three . . . he made it seven seconds before the yips and cries began again. We repeated the exercise several times. Each time it was the same.

I was tired and decided it was time for him to cry himself to sleep. I left the garage light on for him, closed the door, walked to the opposite side of the house, and crawled into bed. The concrete walls didn't muffle his pitiful cries. I lay there, trying to ignore them. I figured he would give up any minute and go to sleep.

The crying continued. Even after I wrapped my pillow around my head, I could still hear it. Poor Marley. Out there alone for the first time in his life. His mother was missing in action, and so were all his brothers and sisters. There wasn't even a single dog *smell*.

I hung on for another half hour before getting up and going to him. As soon as he spotted me, his face brightened and his tail began to beat the side of the box.

It was as if he were saying, "Come on. Hop in. There's plenty of room."

Instead I lifted the box with him in it and carried it into my bedroom. I placed it on the floor against the side of the bed. I lay down on the very edge of the mattress, my arm dangling into the box. There, my hand resting on his side where I could feel his rib cage rise and fall with his every breath, we both drifted off to sleep.

3

Mr. Wiggles

For the next three days I threw myself into taking care of our new puppy. I lay on the floor with him and let him scamper all over me. I wrestled with him. I used an old hand towel to play tug-of-war with him. Boy, was he strong! He followed me everywhere—and tried to gnaw on anything he could get his teeth around.

It took Marley just one day to discover the best thing about his new home—toilet paper. Five seconds after he disappeared into the bathroom, he came racing back out. As he sprinted across the house with the end of the toilet-paper roll clenched in his teeth, a paper ribbon unrolled behind him. The place looked like it had been decorated for Halloween.

Every half hour or so I would lead him into the backyard to pee or poop. When he had accidents in the house, I scolded him. When he peed outside, I placed my cheek against his and praised him in my sweetest voice. And when he pooped outside, I carried on as though we'd just won the lottery.

When Jenny returned from Disney World, she threw herself into him with the same utter abandon. It was amazing. As the days unfolded I saw in my young wife a gentle motherly side I had not known existed. She held him. She petted him. She played with him. She fussed over him. She combed through every strand of his fur in search of fleas and ticks. She rose every couple of hours through the night—night after night—to take him outside for bathroom breaks.

Mostly Jenny fed him.

Following the instructions on the bag, we gave Marley three large bowls of puppy chow a day. He wolfed down every morsel in a matter of seconds. Marley's appetite was huge, and his poop was huger still. The giant mounds that came out looked an awful lot like what he'd eaten earlier. Was he even digesting this stuff?

Apparently he was. Marley was growing at a furious pace. Each day he was a little longer, a little wider, a little taller, a little heavier. He was twenty-one pounds when I brought him home. Within weeks he was up to fifty. His cute little puppy head had rapidly morphed into something resembling the shape and heft of a blacksmith's anvil.

Marley's paws were enormous. His sides already rippled with muscle. His chest was almost as broad as a bulldozer. His little puppy tail was becoming as thick and powerful as an otter's.

What a tail it was. Every last object in our house that was at knee level or below was knocked in all directions by Marley's wildly wagging weapon. He cleared coffee tables, scattered magazines, knocked framed photographs off shelves, and sent bottles and glasses flying. Gradually Jenny and I moved every item to higher ground, safely above the sweep of his swinging mallet.

Marley didn't actually wag his tail. He wagged his whole body, starting with the front shoulders and working backward. He was like the canine version of a

Slinky. We swore there were no bones inside him—just one big, elastic muscle. Jenny began calling him Mr. Wiggles.

Marley wiggled most when he had something in his mouth. His reaction to any situation was the same. He would grab the nearest shoe or pillow or pencil and run with it. Really, any item would do. Some little voice in his head seemed to be whispering to him, "Go ahead! Pick it up! Drool all over it! Run!"

Some of the objects he grabbed were small enough to conceal, and this made him especially pleased. He seemed to think he was getting away with something. But when Marley had something to hide, he couldn't keep it to himself. He would explode into hyperdrive. His body would quiver, his head would bob from side to side, and his entire rear end would swing in a sort of spastic dance. We called it the Marley Mambo.

"All right, what have you got this time?" I'd say.

Marley would waggle his way around the room. His hips swayed and his head flailed up and down like a whinnying horse. He would be so overjoyed with his forbidden prize, he could not contain himself. When I would finally get him cornered and pry open his jaws, I never came up empty-handed. There was always something he had plucked out of the trash or off the floor. As he got taller, he'd take it right off the dining room table. Paper towels, wadded Kleenex, grocery receipts, wine corks, paper clips, chess pieces, bottle caps. It was like a junkyard in there.

Most evenings after dinner Jenny and I strolled together with Marley along the waterfront. *Stroll* is probably the wrong word. Marley strolled like a runaway locomotive strolls. He surged ahead, pulling on his leash with all his might, choking himself hoarse in the process. We yanked him back. He yanked us forward. We tugged. He pulled. He veered left and right, darting to every mailbox and shrub, sniffing, panting, and peeing without fully stopping. He usually and got more pee on himself than on the intended target. He circled behind us, wrapping the leash around our ankles. Then he lurched again, nearly tripping us. When someone approached with another dog, Marley would bolt at them joyously, rearing up on his hind legs when he reached the end of the leash. He just wanted to make friends.

"He sure seems to love life," one dog owner commented. That just about said it all.

4

Master and Beast

Marley was growing up *fast*. When he was small, his skin was so droopy that he looked like he was wearing an oversized yellow fur coat. By the time he was five months old, his body had filled out the wrinkles. His giant puppy paws no longer looked like canine clown feet. His needle-sharp baby teeth had turned into fangs that could destroy a Frisbee in a few quick chomps. His high bark had deepened to a scary boom. When he stood on his hind legs, he could rest his paws on my shoulders and look me straight in the eye.

The first time the vet saw him, he let out a soft whistle and said, "You're going to have a big boy on your hands."

And we did.

We were not the only ones to notice. Our front door had a small oblong window at eye level. Marley lived for company. Whenever someone rang the bell, he would streak across the house. Then he'd go into a full skid as he approached the foyer. Sliding across the wood floors and tossing up throw rugs along the way, he didn't stop until he crashed into the door with a loud thud. At the door, he'd hop up on his hind legs and yelp wildly. His big head filled the tiny window as he stared straight into the face of whoever was on the other side. Terrified strangers ran from "the beast." They raced to the middle of the driveway and waited for someone to answer the door.

After breakfast one morning, Jenny and I decided to walk Marley down to the water for a swim. When we reached the little beach, I wagged a stick in front of Marley's face and took off his leash. He stared at the stick as if he were a starving man staring at a loaf of bread. His eyes never left the prize.

"Go get it!" I shouted, and hurled the stick as far out onto the water as I could. He galloped down the beach. As he entered the shallow water, plumes of spray shot up around him. This is what Labrador retrievers are born to do. It is in their genes.

Labs are known for their desire to fetch. People bred these water dogs to help hunt birds. Once a bird was shot, the dogs would race to get it. Sometimes that meant leaping into ice-cold water to get the dead animal and bring it back to the hunter. These loyal friends never expected a reward for their hard work.

Marley had inherited at least half of the instinct. He was a master at chasing his prey. He didn't quite get that he was supposed to return it. He might as well have said, "If you want the stick back that bad, *you* jump in the water for it."

Marley charged back up onto the beach with his prize in his teeth.

"Bring it here!" I yelled, slapping my hands together. "C'mon, boy, give it to me!" He pranced over, his whole body wagging with excitement, and shaking water and sand all over me.

To my surprise, Marley dropped the stick at my feet. *Wow,* I thought. *How's that for service?* But when I reached down to pick up the stick, Marley was ready. He dove in, grabbed it, and raced across the beach in crazy figure eights. He swerved back, nearly colliding with me, taunting me to chase him. I made a few lunges at him, but he was too fast and agile.

"You're supposed to be a Labrador retriever!" I shouted. "Not a Labrador evader!"

Maybe Marley had strength, but I had brains. I grabbed a second stick and made a big deal about it. I held it over my head and tossed it from hand to hand. I swung it from side to side. He crept closer until he was just inches in front of me. I rubbed the stick across his snout and watched as he went cross-eyed trying to keep it in his sights.

The little cogs turned in his head. He tried to figure out how he could grab the new stick without giving up the old one. His upper lip quivered.

"I wonder if I could make a quick two-for-one grab," he seemed to be asking himself. Soon I had my free hand firmly around the end of the stick in his mouth. I tugged and he tugged back, growling.

I pressed the second stick against his nostrils. "You know you want it," I whispered. And did he ever. The temptation was too much to bear. I could feel his grip loosening. And then he made his move. He opened his jaws to try to grab the second stick without losing the first. In a heartbeat, I whipped both sticks high above my head. He leaped in the air, barking and spinning, obviously at a loss to how such a carefully laid battle plan could have gone so wrong.

"This is why I am the master and you are the beast," I told him.

In response, Marley shook water and sand in my face.

I threw one of the sticks out into the water and he raced after it, yelping madly as he went. When he returned he was a new, wiser opponent. This time he was cautious and refused to come anywhere near me. He stood about ten yards away, stick in mouth, eyeing the new object of his desire. It just happened to be the old object of his desire, his first stick. Now it was perched high above my head. I could see the cogs moving again. He was thinking, "This time I'll just wait right here until he throws it, then he'll have no sticks and I'll have both sticks."

"You think I'm really dumb, don't you, dog?" I said. I heaved back and hurled the stick with all my might. Marley roared into the water with his stick still locked in his teeth. The only thing was, I hadn't let go of mine. Do you think Marley figured that out? He swam halfway across the water before catching on that the stick was still in my hand.

"You're cruel!" Jenny yelled down from her bench, laughing.

When Marley finally got back onshore, he plopped down in the sand. Although he was exhausted, he was not about to give up his stick. I showed him mine and reminded him how much better it was than his.

"Drop it!" I ordered. I cocked my arm back as if to throw. The dumb dog bolted back to his feet and began heading for the water again. "Drop it!" I repeated when he returned. It took several tries, but finally he did just that. And the instant his stick hit the sand, I launched mine into the air for him. We did it over and over, and each time he seemed to understand a little more clearly. Slowly the lesson was sinking into that thick skull of his. If he returned his stick to me, I would throw a new one for him.

"You've got to give to get," I told him. He leaped up and gave me a sloppy, sandy kiss. I guess that meant he'd learned his lesson.

As Jenny and I walked home, the tuckered Marley

for once did not strain against his leash. "You know," I said to Jenny, "I really think he's starting to get it."

Jenny looked down at him plodding along beside us. He was soaking wet and coated in sand, spittle foaming on his lips. He clenched his prize stick in his jaws.

"I wouldn't be so sure of that," she said.

5

A Battle of Wills

When Marley was not quite six months old, we signed him up for obedience classes. He definitely needed them. Despite his stick-fetching breakthrough on the beach that day, he was proving himself a challenging student—dense, wild, and constantly distracted. We were beginning to figure out that he was not like other dogs. We needed professional help.

Our veterinarian told us about a local dog-training club that offered basic obedience classes. When we went to register Marley, we met the woman who would be teaching our class. She was a stern, no-nonsense dog trainer who believed that there are no bad dogs, only weak-willed and hapless owners.

As Jenny, Marley, and I arrived for the first lesson, Marley spotted the other dogs gathering with their owners across the tarmac.

"A party!" he barked. He leaped over us and out of the car. He was off in a tear, his leash dragging behind him. He darted from one dog to the next, sniffing private parts, dribbling pee, and flinging huge wads of spit through the air. Sniff sniff. Dribble dribble. Fling fling. For Marley it was a festival of smells. He stayed just ahead of me as I raced after him. Each time I was nearly upon him, he would scoot a few feet farther away.

I finally got close. Taking a giant leap, I landed hard with both feet on the leash. He stopped with a sudden jerk. For a second, I was convinced I'd broken his neck. He jerked backward, landed on his back, flipped around, and gazed up at me with the serene expression of a kid who has just eaten every last piece of candy in the candy store.

Meanwhile, the instructor was staring at us as if I had thrown off my clothes and danced naked right there on the blacktop. She was not amused.

"Take your place, please," she said curtly. Jenny and I tugged Marley into position. "You are going to have to decide which of you is going to be the trainer," she added.

The instructor didn't understand that we both wanted to participate so each of us could work with him at home. I decided to explain.

"But we—" I began.

"A dog can only answer to one master," she said, cutting me off.

"But—" I said. This time her glare silenced me. I slunk to the sidelines with my tail between my legs, leaving Master Jenny in command.

This was probably a mistake. Marley was already way stronger than Jenny and knew it. The instructor began her introduction on the importance of establishing dominance over our pets. That's when Marley spotted the standard poodle on the opposite side of the class. He lunged off, with Jenny in tow.

All the other dogs sat ten feet apart, beside their masters. They waited for instructions. Jenny was fighting to plant her feet and bring Marley to a halt.

"Forward ho!" Marley seemed to be telling her. He lumbered on and tugged her across the parking lot in pursuit of hot poodle butt-sniffing action. Jenny looked like a water-skier being towed behind a powerboat. Everyone stared. Some snickered. I covered my eyes.

Marley crashed into the poodle. Everyone waited as he sniffed every inch of her. I imagined it was his way of saying, "Nice to meet you!" Jenny tugged with all of her might, but Marley ignored her. "I'm not done yet," he seemed to be saying. Finally he finished saying his hellos, and Jenny was able to drag him back into place.

"That, class, is an example of a dog that has been allowed to think he is the alpha male of his pack," the instructor announced calmly. "Right now, he's in charge." Marley agreed by attacking his tail, spinning wildly as his jaws snapped at thin air. In the process he wrapped the leash around Jenny's ankles until she was fully immobilized. I winced and was thankful that it wasn't me out there.

The instructor showed the class how to command dogs to sit.

"Sit!" Jenny ordered. Marley jumped on her and put his paws on her shoulders. She pressed his butt to the ground. He rolled over for a belly rub. She tried to tug him into place. He grabbed the leash in his teeth, shaking his head from side to side as if he were wrestling a python.

It was too painful to watch. At one point, I opened my eyes to see Jenny lying on the pavement facedown. Marley stood over her, panting happily. She later told me she was trying to show him the down command.

Class ended, and Jenny and Marley rejoined me. So did the teacher.

"You really need to get control over that animal," she said with a sneer.

"Well, thank you for that valuable advice. Actually, we signed up just to make the rest of the class laugh." At least, that's what I wanted to say. Actually, neither of us breathed a word. We just retreated to the car in humiliation and drove home in silence. The only sound was Marley's loud, excited panting.

Finally I broke the silence. "He sure loves school!" I said.

The next week Marley and I were back, but this time without Jenny. When I suggested to her that I was probably the closest thing to an alpha dog we were going to find in our home, she gladly relinquished her brief title as master and commander. Before leaving the house, I flipped Marley over on his back, towered over him, and growled in my most intimidating voice, "I'm the boss! You're not the boss! I'm the boss! Got it, Alpha Dog?" He thumped his tail on the floor and tried to gnaw on my wrists.

The night's lesson was walking on heel. I was eager to master it. I was tired of fighting Marley every step of every walk. Jenny was, too. Once he took off after a cat and yanked her off her feet, leaving her with bloody knees. It was time he learned to trot by our sides.

I wrestled him to our spot on the tarmac, pulling him back from every dog we passed along the way.

"Class, on the count of three," the instructor called out. "One . . . two . . . three."

"Marley, heel!" I commanded. As soon as I took my first step, he shot off like a fighter jet from an aircraft carrier. I yanked back hard on the leash. He coughed and gasped as the collar tightened around his airway. He sprang back for an instant, then lunged forward again. I yanked back. He gasped again. We continued like this the entire length of the parking lot. He was coughing and panting. I was grunting and sweating.

"Rein that dog in!" the instructor yelled. I tried with all my might, but the lesson wasn't sinking in. I thought that Marley might just strangle himself before he figured it out. Meanwhile, the other dogs were prancing along at their owners' sides.

The instructor had the class line up and try again. Once again, Marley lurched like a maniac across the blacktop. With his eyes bulging, he strangled himself as he went.

"Here," the instructor said impatiently. "Let me show you." I handed the leash to her. She tugged Marley around into position. She pulled up on the collar as she ordered him to sit. Sure enough, he sat, eagerly looking up at her.

With a yank of the leash, the instructor set off with him. Almost instantly he barreled ahead as if he were pulling the lead sled in a dogsled race. She corrected hard, pulling him off balance. He stumbled, wheezed, then lunged forward again. It looked like he was going to pull her arm out of its socket. I should have been embarrassed. But I felt an odd sort of satisfaction. She wasn't having any more success than I was. My classmates snickered, and I beamed with perverse pride. I wanted to yell, "See, my dog is awful for everyone, not just me!"

I had to admit, the scene was pretty hilarious. The two of them reached the end of the parking lot. Then they turned and lurched back toward us.

The instructor scowled. Marley was joyous beyond words. She yanked furiously at the leash. Slobbering with excitement, Marley yanked back harder still. I could tell what he was thinking. "All right! Tug-of-war."

When Marley saw me, he hit the gas. Filled with near-supernatural speed, he made a dash for me. The instructor broke into a sprint to keep from being pulled off her feet. Marley didn't stop until he slammed into me with his usual exuberance.

The instructor shot me a look that told me I was in trouble. Marley had made a mockery of her class. He had publicly humiliated her.

The instructor handed the leash back to me. "Okay, class, on the count of three . . . ," she said, pretending the whole thing hadn't even happened.

When the lesson was over, she asked if I could stay after for a minute. "I think your dog is still a little young for structured obedience training," she explained.

"He's a handful, isn't he?" I said. Now that we had shared the same humiliating experience, I felt as though we were friends.

"He's simply not ready for this," she said. "He has some growing up to do."

It was beginning to dawn on me what she was getting at. "Are you trying to tell me—"

"He's a distraction to the other dogs."

"—that you're—"

"He's just too excitable."

"—kicking us out of class?"

"You can always bring him back in another six or eight months."

"So you're kicking us out?"

"I'll happily give you a full refund."

"You're kicking us out."

"Yes," she finally said. "I'm kicking you out."

Marley lifted his leg and let loose a raging stream of pee, nearly hitting his beloved instructor's foot.

Sometimes a man needs to get angry to get serious. The instructor had made me angry. I owned a beautiful, purebred Labrador retriever, a proud member of the breed famous for its ability to guide the blind, rescue disaster victims, assist hunters, and pluck fish from big ocean swells, all with calm intelligence. How dare she write him off after just two lessons? Okay, he was a bit on the spirited side, but his intentions were all good.

I was going to prove to that insufferable stuffed shirt that she could kick us out but Marley was no quitter. He would show her!

First thing the next morning, Marley was out in the

backyard with me. "Nobody kicks the Grogan boys out of obedience school," I told him. "Untrainable? We'll see who's untrainable. Right?" He bounced up and down. "Can we do it, Marley?" He wiggled. "I can't hear you! Can we do it?" He yelped. "That's better. Now let's get to work."

We started with the sit command, which I had been practicing with him since he was a small puppy. He was already quite good at it. I towered over him and gave him my best alpha-dog scowl.

"Sit," I said in a firm but calm voice. He sat. "Good boy!" I praised.

We repeated the exercise several times. Next we moved to the down command, another one I had been practicing with him. He stared intently into my eyes, neck straining forward, anticipating my directive.

I slowly raised my hand in the air and held it there as he waited for the word. With a sharp downward motion, I snapped my fingers, pointed at the ground and said, "Down!" Marley collapsed in a heap, hitting the ground with a thud. He went down with gusto—as if a mortar shell had just exploded behind him.

Jenny, sitting on the porch with her coffee, noticed it, too. "Incoming!" she yelled out.

After several rounds of hit-the-deck, I moved up to the next challenge—come on command. This was a tough one for Marley. The coming part was not the problem; it was waiting in place until we called him. He was so anxious to be plastered against us that he could not sit still while we walked away from him.

"Sit," I commanded. He faced me, and I fixed my eyes on his. As we stared at each other, I raised my palm, holding it out in front of me like a crossing guard. "Stay," I said, and took a step backward. He froze, staring anxiously, waiting for the slightest sign he could join me. On my fourth step backward, he could take it no longer and broke free, racing up and tumbling against me. I scolded him and tried it again. And again and again.

Each time he allowed me to get a little farther away before charging. Eventually I stood fifty feet across the yard, with my palm out toward him. I stood and waited. He sat, locked in position, his entire body quaking with anticipation. I could see the nervous energy building in him. He was like a volcano ready to blow. But he stayed. I counted to ten. He did not budge. His eyes froze on me. His muscles bulged. Okay, enough torture.

I dropped my hand and yelled, "Marley, come!"

As he catapulted forward, I squatted down and

clapped my hands to encourage him. I thought he might go racing willy-nilly across the yard, but he made a beeline straight for me. *Perfect!* I thought.

"C'mon, boy! C'mon!" I coached. He was barreling right at me. "Slow it down, boy," I said. He just kept coming. "Slow down!" He had this vacant, crazed look on his face. It was a one-dog stampede. I had time for one final command. "STOP!" I screamed.

Blam! He plowed into me without breaking stride. I pitched backward, slamming hard to the ground. When I opened my eyes a few seconds later, he was straddling me with all four paws, lying on my chest and desperately licking my face.

"How did I do, boss?" my proud puppy seemed to be asking.

Technically speaking, he had followed orders exactly. After all, I had failed to mention anything about stopping once he got to me.

"Mission accomplished," I said with a groan.

Jenny peered out the kitchen window. "I'm off to work," she shouted. "When you two are done making out, don't forget to close the windows. It's supposed to rain this afternoon." I gave Linebacker Dog a snack and then showered and headed off myself to my job as a newspaper reporter.

When I arrived home that night, Jenny was waiting for me at the front door. I could tell she was upset.

"Go look in the garage," she said.

I opened the door into the garage, and the first thing I spotted was Marley, lying on his carpet, looking sad.

My mind took a photo of the scene. Marley's snout and front paws were not right. They were dark brown, not their usual light yellow. It took me a few seconds to figure out that they were covered in dried blood. Then my focus zoomed out and I sucked in my breath. We had thought the garage was indestructible, but Marley had destroyed it. Throw rugs were shredded. Paint was clawed off the concrete walls. The ironing board was tipped over, its fabric cover hanging in ribbons.

Worst of all, the doorway in which I stood looked like it had been attacked with a chipper-shredder. Bits of wood were sprayed in a ten-foot semicircle around the door, which had a hole halfway through to the other side. The bottom three feet of the doorjamb were missing entirely and nowhere to be found. Blood streaked the walls from where Marley had shredded his paws and muzzle.

"I don't believe it," I said, more amazed than angry.

"When I came home for lunch, everything was fine," Jenny said from behind me. "But I could tell it was getting ready to rain." After she was back at work, an intense storm had moved through, bringing with it sheets of rain and dazzling flashes of lightning. The thunder was so powerful, you could actually feel it thump against your chest.

While the storm raged, Marley had desperately tried to escape. The storm had sent him into a complete, panic-stricken frenzy. Alone and terrified as the storm came, Marley had decided his best chance at survival was to begin digging his way into the house. When Jenny arrived home a couple hours later, Marley stood in the middle of the mess he had made.

But it didn't take long for Marley to forget the whole incident. Back to his old self, he grabbed a chew toy and bounced around us, looking for a little tug-of-war action. I held him still while Jenny sponged the blood off his fur. Then he watched us, tail wagging, as we cleaned up his handiwork.

"You don't have to look so happy about it." I scowled and brought him inside for the night.

6

The Great Escape

One thing was clear. Jenny and I loved our dog, but having a bunch of little Marleys running around in the world was not a good idea. It was time to make sure Marley couldn't make any puppies. Jenny and I decided to have him fixed so he would never be a father.

As we got ready to take Marley to the vet, he bounced happily off the walls. "Yippee!" his excited movements told us. He could tell he was going for a car ride, and he didn't care where.

For Marley, any trip was a good trip. It didn't matter where we were going or for how long. Take out the trash? "No problem!" Walk to the corner for a gallon of milk? "Count me in!"

When I whistled, Marley bounded out the door and into the car. He was revved up and ready to go. Jenny drove and I sat in the passenger seat. From the backseat Marley balanced his front paws on the center console— just like he always did. His nose touched the rearview mirror. Every time Jenny pressed the brakes, he went crashing into the windshield. Marley didn't care. He was riding shotgun with his two best friends.

"Life doesn't get any better than this," his puppy joy announced.

I rolled down my window a bit and Marley leaned against me, trying to catch a whiff of the outdoor smells. Soon he squirmed his way fully onto my lap. He pressed his nose so firmly into the narrow crack of the window that he snorted each time he tried to inhale.

"Do you want a little more fresh air, buddy?" I asked. I opened the window wide enough for him to stick out his snout. He was enjoying the sensation so much, I opened it farther. Soon his entire head was out the window. His tongue hung out and his ears flapped behind him in the wind. Was he happy!

As we drove down the highway, Jenny and I talked. Pretty soon I noticed that Marley had hooked both of his front paws over the edge of the half-open window. And now his neck and upper shoulders were hanging out of the car, too. He just needed a pair of goggles and a silk scarf to look like one of those World War I flying aces.

"John, he's making me nervous," Jenny said.

"He's fine," I answered. "He just wants a little fresh—"

At that instant he slid his front legs out the window until his armpits were resting on the edge of the glass.

"John, grab him! Grab him!" Jenny yelled.

Before I could do anything, Marley was scrambling out the window of our moving car. His butt was up in the air, and his hind legs were clawing for something to hold on to. He was making his break!

As his body slithered past me, I lunged for him and managed to grab the end of his tail with my left hand. Jenny was braking hard even though there was traffic all around us. Marley's entire body dangled outside the moving car, hanging upside down by his tail. My body was twisted around, and I couldn't get my other hand on him. Marley was frantically trotting along with his front paws on the pavement.

Jenny stopped the car in the left-hand lane. Cars lined up behind us. Their horns blared.

"Now what?" I yelled. I was stuck. I couldn't pull him back in the window. I couldn't open the door. I couldn't get my other arm out. And I didn't dare let go of him—I was convinced he'd dash in the path of one of the angry drivers swerving around us. With my face scrunched against the glass, I held on for dear life.

Jenny put on the car's flashers and ran around to my side. She grabbed Marley and held him by the collar until I could get out and help her wrestle him back into the car.

All the action had taken place directly in front of a gas station. As Jenny got the car moving again, I looked over to see that all the mechanics had come out to take in the show. I thought they were going to pee in their pants, they were laughing so hard.

"Thanks, guys!" I called out. "Glad we could brighten your morning."

7

The Things He Ate

Before long, Jenny and I were expecting our first child. Marley would stop being the baby of the family, and we had to prepare him for the change. So every day we worked on his training.

Now I was able to entertain our friends by yelling, "Incoming!" and watching Marley crash to the floor, all four limbs splayed.

He always came on command—unless something caught his attention, such as another dog, squirrel, butterfly, mailman, or floating weed seed. He always sat—unless he felt like standing. He always heeled—unless there was something so tempting it was worth strangling himself over, such as another dog, squirrel, butterfly. . . . Well, you get the idea.

Marley's training was coming along. But that didn't mean he was mellowing into a calm, well-behaved dog. If I towered over him and barked stern orders, he would obey. Sometimes he'd even do it eagerly. But Marley was still Marley. And Marley was incorrigible.

A giant mango tree grew in our Florida backyard, and mangoes rained down to the ground. Marley could never eat enough. Each weighed a pound or more. They were so sweet they could make your teeth ache. Marley would stretch out in the grass, anchor a ripe mango between his front paws, and remove every bit of flesh from the skin. It was as if he were performing surgery. He would hold the large pits in his mouth like lozenges. When he finally spit them out, they looked like they had been cleaned in an acid bath. There was not a speck of fruit left on them. Some days he would be out there for hours, frantically gobbling down mango after mango.

When you eat lots of fruit, you get lots of poop.

Soon our backyard was littered with large piles of fes-
tively colored dog droppings. The one advantage to this
was that it was nearly impossible to accidentally step in
a heap of his poop, which glowed like orange traffic
cones.

Mangoes weren't the only item coming out in the
poop piles. Marley also ate other things, and these, too,
came out the other end. I saw the evidence each morning as I shoveled up his piles. Here a shoelace, there a
rubber band. In one load a mangled soda-bottle top. In
another the gnawed cap to a ballpoint pen.

"So that's where my comb went!" I exclaimed one
morning.

Marley ate bath towels, sponges, socks, and used
Kleenex. Handi Wipes were one of his favorites. When
they came out, they looked like little blue flags marking
each fluorescent mango mountain.

Not everything went down easily, and Marley vomited easily and often.

Gaaaaack! When we heard the noise, we knew
Marley had puked. By the time we rushed into the
room, there would be another household item, sitting
in a puddle of half-digested mangoes and dog chow.
Marley never puked on the hardwood floors or even the

kitchen linoleum if he could help it. He always aimed for the fancy rug.

Jenny and I decided that it would be nice to have a dog we could trust to be alone in the house. We were tired of locking him in the garage every time we stepped out. And as Jenny said, "What's the point of having a dog if he can't greet you at the door when you get home?"

We began leaving him briefly while we ran to the store or dropped by a neighbor's house. When he behaved himself, he would push his black nose through the miniblinds and stare out the living room window, waiting for us. When he hadn't behaved, he hid.

Once we were gone for less than an hour. Marley was under the bed. (And at his size, he really had to work to get under there.) He looked like he'd just murdered the mailman. The house seemed fine, but we knew he was hiding some dark secret. Guilt radiated off him like heat off the sun. We walked from room to room, trying to figure out what he had done wrong. Then I noticed that the foam cover to one of the stereo speakers was missing. We looked everywhere for it. It was gone without a trace. Marley nearly got away with it. But I found evidence of his guilt when I went on poop patrol the next morning. Pieces of the speaker cover surfaced for days.

During our next outing, Marley removed the woofer cone from the same speaker. The speaker wasn't knocked over. It wasn't out of place at all. The part was simply gone, as if someone had sliced it with a razor blade. Eventually he got around to doing the same to the other speaker.

Another time, he turned our four-legged footstool into a three-legged footstool. Not a single splinter was left.

We swore it could never snow in South Florida, but one day we opened the front door to find a blizzard in the living room. The air was filled with soft white fluff floating down. We spotted Marley in front of the fireplace, half buried in a snowdrift, violently shaking a large feather pillow from side to side as though he had just captured an ostrich.

For the most part we accepted the damage. After all, in every dog owner's life a few precious items get chewed, broken, or totally destroyed. One time, though, I was desperate. I was ready to do whatever it took to get what was mine—or Jenny's, actually.

For her birthday I had bought Jenny an eighteen-karat gold necklace, a delicate chain with a tiny clasp.

She immediately put it on.

A few hours later she pressed her hand to her throat. "My necklace!" she screamed. "It's gone."

"Don't panic," I told her. "We haven't left the house. It's got to be right here somewhere." We began scouring the house, room by room. As we searched, I gradually became aware that Marley was more rambunctious than usual. I straightened up and looked at him. He was squirming like a centipede. When he noticed I had him in my sights, he began evasive action. *Oh, no,* I thought, *the Marley Mambo.* It could mean only one thing.

"What's that," Jenny asked, panic rising in her voice, "hanging out of his mouth?"

It was thin and delicate. And gold. "Oh, shoot!" I said.

"Don't make any sudden moves," she ordered, her voice dropping to a whisper. We both froze.

"Okay, boy, it's all right," I coaxed like a hostage negotiator on a SWAT team. "We're not mad at you. Come on now. We just want the necklace back." Instinctively Jenny and I began to circle him from opposite directions, moving as slowly as glaciers. It was as if he were wired with high explosives and one false move could set him off.

"Easy, Marley," Jenny said in her calmest voice.

"Easy now. Drop the necklace and no one gets hurt."

Marley eyed us suspiciously, his head darting back and forth between us. We had him cornered, but he knew he had something we wanted. I could see him weighing his options. What did he want? A ransom, perhaps? I expected him to say, "Leave two hundred unmarked Milk-Bones in a plain paper bag or you'll never see your precious little necklace again."

"Drop it, Marley," I whispered, taking another small step forward. His whole body began to wag. I crept forward inch by inch. Jenny closed in from the side. We were within striking distance. We glanced at each other and knew, without speaking, what to do. We had been through this many times before. She would lunge for the hindquarters, pinning his back legs to prevent escape. I would lunge for the head, prying open his jaws and nabbing the contraband. With any luck, we'd be in and out in a matter of seconds.

That was the plan, and Marley saw it coming.

We were less than two feet away from him. I nodded to Jenny. *"On three,"* I silently mouthed.

Marley threw his head back and made a loud smacking sound. The tail end of the chain, which had been dangling out of his mouth, disappeared.

"He's eating it!" Jenny screamed. Together we dove at him. Jenny tackled him by the hind legs. I gripped him in a headlock, forced his jaws open, and pushed my whole hand into his mouth and down his throat. I probed every flap and crevice but came up empty.

"It's too late," I said. "He swallowed it."

"Cough it up!" Jenny yelled, slapping him on the back.

"*Buuuuurrrp!*" Marley answered.

Marley may have won the battle, but we knew it was just a matter of time before we won the war. Nature's call was on our side. Sooner or later, what went in had to come out. I knew if I poked through his poop long enough, I would find it. It was a disgusting thought, but grossed out or not, I was going in.

And so I prepared Marley his favorite laxative—a giant bowl of sliced mangoes. Then I settled in for the long wait. For three days I followed him around every time I let him out, eagerly waiting to swoop in with my shovel. Instead of tossing his piles over the fence, I carefully placed each on a wide board in the grass. I poked it with a tree branch while I sprayed with a garden hose. The poop washed away into the grass. Anything that wasn't poop stayed behind. I felt like a gold miner coming up with a treasure trove of swallowed junk, from shoelaces to guitar picks. But no necklace.

Where was it? Shouldn't it have come out by now? I began wondering if I had missed it, accidentally washing it into the grass. If I had, it would remain lost forever. But how could I miss a twenty-inch gold chain?

On the fourth day, my patience paid off.

I scooped up Marley's latest deposit. "I can't believe I'm doing this," I said. I began poking and spraying. As the poop melted away, I searched for any sign of the necklace. Nothing. I was about to give up when I spotted something odd—a small brown lump, about the size of a lima bean. It wasn't even close to being large enough to be the missing jewelry, yet clearly it did not seem to belong there. I pinned it down with my probing branch and gave the object a strong blast from the hose nozzle. As the water washed it clean, I got a glimmer of something exceptionally bright and shiny. Eureka! I had struck gold.

The necklace was much smaller than I would have guessed possible. It was as though some unknown alien power had sucked it into a mysterious dimension of space and time before spitting it out again. And, actually, that wasn't too far from the truth. The strong

stream of water began to loosen the hard wad, and gradually the lump of gold unraveled back to its original
shape, untangled and unmangled. Good as new. No,
actually better than new. I took it inside to show Jenny,
who was overjoyed to have it back. She didn't care
where it had been. We both marveled at how blindingly
bright it was now—far more dazzling than when it had
gone in. Marley's stomach acids had done an amazing
job. It was the most brilliant gold I had ever seen.

"Man," I said with a whistle. "We should open a
jewelry-cleaning business."

"It's got possibilities, Grogan," Jenny said, and went
off to disinfect her recovered birthday present. She wore
that gold chain for years. Every time I looked at it I had
the same vivid flashback. My stick and I had gone
where no man had ever gone before. And none should
ever go again.

8

The Dog's Got to Go

By 1993, Marley wasn't the only one keeping us on our toes. We now also had two human babies—Patrick and Conor. We rarely slept through the night, and Jenny spent her days keeping the boys happy. Between their demands and Marley's antics, she was exhausted. Eventually Marley's bad behavior just wasn't funny anymore.

One day I opened the front door to find Jenny crying uncontrollably and yelling at Marley.

"Why? Why do you do this?" Jenny screamed at

him. "Why do you wreck everything?"

In that instant I saw what he had done. The couch cushion was gouged open, the fabric shredded and the stuffing pulled out. She was so upset that she started pounding on him with her fists, more like she was beating a kettledrum than trying to hurt him. Marley stood with head down and legs spread. He looked as though he were leaning into a hurricane. He didn't try to flee or dodge the blows. He just stood there and took each one without a whimper or complaint.

"Hey! Hey! Hey!" I shouted, grabbing Jenny's wrists. "Come on. Stop. Stop!" She was sobbing and gasping for breath. "Stop," I repeated.

I stepped between her and Marley and shoved my face directly in front of hers. It was like a stranger was staring back at me. I did not recognize the look in her eyes. "Get him out of here," she said, her voice flat and tinged with a quiet burn. "Get him out of here now."

"Okay, I'll take him out," I said, "but you settle down."

"Get him out of here and keep him out of here," she said.

I opened the front door and he bounded outside. When I turned back to grab his leash off the table,

Jenny said, "I mean it. I want him gone. I want him out of here for good."

"Come on," I said. "You don't mean that."

"I mean it," she said. "I'm done with that dog. You find him a new home, or I will."

Jenny couldn't mean it. She loved this dog. She adored him despite his long list of shortcomings. She was upset. She was stressed to the breaking point. She would reconsider. Wouldn't she? One thing was clear—she needed time to cool down.

I walked out the door without another word. In the front yard, Marley raced around, jumping into the air and snapping his jaws, trying to bite the leash out of my hand. He was his old jolly self. I knew Jenny hadn't hurt him. I whacked him much harder when I played rough with him. He loved it and always bounded back for more. He was an unstoppable machine of muscle and strength that barely felt pain.

Once when I was in the driveway washing the car, he'd jammed his head into the bucket of soapy water. He galloped blindly off across the front lawns with the bucket and crashed full force into a concrete wall. It didn't seem to faze him.

Even though he was a big dense oaf, Marley did have

an incredibly sensitive streak. If someone got angry and slapped him lightly on the rump or even just spoke to him with a stern voice, he acted deeply wounded.

Jenny hadn't hurt Marley physically, not even close, but she had crushed his feelings. One of his two best pals in the whole world had just turned on him. She was his mistress and he was her faithful companion. He figured that if she needed to strike him, he needed to suck it up and take it. As far as dogs went, he was not good at much. But he was unquestionably loyal. Now it was my job to repair the damage and make things right again.

Out on the street, I hooked him to his leash. "Sit!" I ordered. He sat. I pulled the choke chain up high on his throat in preparation for our walk. Before I stepped off I ran my hand over his head and massaged his neck. He flipped his nose in the air and looked up at me, his tongue hanging halfway down his neck. He had forgotten all about what had happened with Jenny. I hoped she had, too.

"What am I going to do with you, you big dope?" I asked him. He leaped straight up, as though he had springs on his paws, and smashed his tongue against my lips.

Marley and I walked for miles that evening, and when I finally opened the front door, he was exhausted and ready to collapse quietly in the corner. Jenny was feeding Patrick a jar of baby food as she cradled Conor in her lap. She was calm. *Whew!* I thought. Back to her old self.

I unleashed Marley, and he took a huge drink. Water sloshed like little tidal waves over the side of his bowl. I toweled up the floor and stole a glance in Jenny's direction. She didn't seem upset at all. Maybe the horrible moment had passed. Maybe she had reconsidered. Maybe she felt sheepish about her outburst and was searching for the words to apologize. I walked past her, with Marley close at my heels.

"I'm dead serious," she said without looking at me. "I want him out of here."

I was not ready to give up on Marley.

To make Jenny happy, I started looking for a new home for him. At the same time, I began the most serious training Marley had ever gotten. My own private Mission: Impossible was to rehabilitate this dog and prove to Jenny he was worthy. I began rising at dawn. With Patrick in the jogging stroller, I headed down to the water to put Marley through the paces.

Sit. Stay. Down. Heel. Over and over we practiced. I was desperate, and Marley seemed to sense it. The stakes were different now—this was for real.

"We're not messing around here, Marley," I told him. "This is it. Let's go." And I put him through the commands again.

"Waddy! Hee-O!" Patrick clapped and called to his big yellow friend.

I couldn't do it alone. Even as I searched the want ads for a new home for him, I reenrolled Marley in obedience school. He was a different dog from the juvenile delinquent I had shown up with the first time around. He was still as wild as a boar, but this time he knew I was the boss and he was the underling. This time there would be no lunges toward other dogs—or at least not many. No out-of-control surges across the tarmac. No crashing into strangers.

For eight weeks I kept him on a tight leash and marched him through the commands. He was overjoyed to cooperate.

The trainer was the exact opposite of the first instructor we had had. At our final meeting, she called us forward. "Okay," she said, "show us what you've got."

"Sit," I ordered. Marley dropped neatly to his backside.

I raised the choke chain high around his throat and tugged on his lead. "Heel!" I commanded. I trotted across the parking lot and back with Marley at my side. His shoulder brushed my calf, just as it was supposed to.

"Sit," I ordered again. I stood directly in front of him and pointed my finger at his forehead. "Stay," I said calmly. With the other hand I dropped his leash. I stepped backward several paces. His big brown eyes fixed on me, waiting for any small sign from me to release him, but he remained anchored. I walked in a circle around him. He quivered with excitement and tried to rotate his head to watch me, but he did not budge.

When I was back in front of him, I decided to have a little fun. I snapped my fingers and yelled, "Incoming!" He hit the deck. The teacher burst out laughing. That was a good sign. I turned my back on him and walked thirty feet away. I could feel his eyes burning into my back, but he didn't move. He was quaking violently by the time I turned around to face him. Marley the Volcano was getting ready to blow.

I spread my feet into a wide boxer's stance in anticipation of what was coming. "Marley . . . ," I said. I let his name hang in the air for a few seconds. "Come!" He shot at me with everything he had, and I braced for the impact. At the last instant I stepped to the side like a bullfighter. He blasted past me, then circled back and goosed me from behind with his nose.

"Good boy, Marley," I gushed, dropping to my knees. "Good, good, good boy! You're a good boy!" He danced around me like we had just climbed to the top of Mount Everest together.

At the end of the evening, the instructor called us up and handed us our diploma. Marley had passed basic obedience training, ranking seventh in the class. So what if it was a class of eight and the eighth dog was a crazy pit bull? I would take it. Marley, my untrainable, undisciplined bad-boy dog, had passed. I was so proud I could have cried. In fact I actually might have, if Marley hadn't leaped up and eaten his diploma.

On the way home, I sang "We Are the Champions" at the top of my lungs. Sensing my joy and pride, Marley stuck his slimy tongue in my ear. For once, I didn't even mind.

9

The Final Round

There was still one piece of unfinished business between Marley and me. I needed to break him of his worst habit of all—jumping on people. It didn't matter if it was a friend or a stranger, a child or an adult, the meter reader or the UPS driver. Marley greeted them the same way. He charged them at full speed, slid across the floor, leaped up, and planted his two front paws on the person's chest or shoulders as he licked their face. When he was a cuddly puppy, it had been cute. Now it was obnoxious, even terrifying. He had knocked over children, startled guests, dirtied our friends' clothes, and nearly taken down my frail mother. No one appreciated it.

Although I had tried breaking him of his habit, regular dog-obedience techniques hadn't worked. The message was not getting through.

"You want to break him of that?" asked a dog owner I respected. "Give him a swift knee in the chest next time he jumps up on you."

"I don't want to hurt him," I said.

"You won't hurt him. A few good jabs with your knee, and I guarantee you he'll be done jumping."

It was tough-love time. Marley had to reform or relocate.

I put my plan into action the next night. "I'm home!" I yelled when I walked in from work.

As usual, Marley came barreling across the wood floors to greet me. He slid the last ten feet as though on ice. Then he lifted off to smash his paws into my chest and slurp at my face.

Bam! Just as his paws made contact with me, I gave one swift pump of my knee. I aimed for the soft spot just below his rib cage. Marley gasped slightly and slid down to the floor, looking up at me with a wounded expression.

"What's your problem?" I could almost hear him say. He had been jumping on me his whole life. What was with the sudden sneak attack?

The next night I repeated the punishment. He leaped. I kneed. He dropped to the floor, coughing. I felt a little cruel, but if I was going to save him, I knew I had to drive home the point.

"Sorry, guy," I said, leaning down so he could lick me with all four paws on the ground. "It's for your own good."

The third night when I walked in, he came charging around the corner, going into his high-speed skid. This time, however, he changed the routine. Instead of leaping, he kept his paws on the ground and crashed head-first into my knees, nearly knocking me over. Yes! Victory!

"You did it, Marley! You did it! Good boy! You didn't jump up," I praised. And I got on my knees so he could slobber me. I was impressed.

The problem was not exactly solved, however. He may have been cured of jumping on me, but he was not cured of jumping on anyone else. The dog was smart enough to figure out that only I posed a threat. He could still jump on the rest of the human race. I needed a plan.

I asked a good friend of mine from work to help me out. Jim Tolpin was a small, mild-mannered man with glasses. If there was anyone Marley thought he could jump up on without consequence, it was Jim.

At the office one day, I laid out the plan. He was to come to the house after work, ring the doorbell, and then walk in. When Marley jumped up to kiss him, he was to give him all he had. "Don't be shy about it," I coached.

That night Jim rang the bell and walked in the door. Sure enough, Marley took the bait and raced at him, ears flying back. When Marley left the ground to leap up on him, Jim took my advice to heart. He kneed Marley right in the soft spot below his ribs, knocking the wind out of him. You could hear the thud across the room. Marley let out a loud moan, went bug-eyed, and sprawled on the floor.

"Have you been studying kung fu?" I asked.

"You told me to make him feel it," he answered.

He had. Marley got to his feet, caught his breath, and greeted Jim the way a dog should—on all four paws. If he could have talked, I swear Marley would have cried "Uncle." Marley never again jumped up on anyone, at least not in my presence, and no one ever kneed him in the chest or anywhere else again.

Gradually Jenny found it in her heart to forgive Marley for all his misdeeds. One morning she woke up and it was like she had completely forgotten about her threat to send him away. With a baby in each arm, Jenny leaned to kiss him. She threw him sticks and made him gravy from hamburger drippings. She danced him around the room when a good song came on the stereo. Sometimes at night when he was calm, I would find her lying on the floor with him, her head resting on his neck.

Our new and improved dog was here to stay.

10

The Audition

Some things in life are so weird they have to be true. So when Jenny called me at the office to tell me Marley was getting a film audition, I knew she couldn't be making it up. Still, I was in disbelief.

"A what?" I asked.

"A film audition."

"Like for a movie?"

"Yes, like for a movie, dumbo," she said. "A feature-length movie."

"Marley? A feature-length movie? Our Marley?" I asked one more time, just to be sure.

It had all started out very simply. A New York film company was making a movie and wanted to see how a typical Florida family lived. They asked if they could photograph our home.

A woman named Colleen came over and started photographing. She took pictures of *everything*—the way we dressed, the way we wore our hair, the way we slouched on the couch. She photographed toothbrushes on the sink. She photographed the babies in their cribs. She photographed our dog, too. Or at least what she could catch of him on film.

"He's a bit of a blur," she said.

Marley could not have been happier to participate. Ever since babies had invaded, Marley ate up all the affection he could get. Colleen could have jabbed him with a cattle prod. As long as he was getting some attention, he was okay with it. Being a lover of large animals and not intimidated by saliva showers, Colleen gave him plenty. She dropped to her knees to wrestle with him.

When she was done, Colleen thanked us and left. We didn't expect to hear from her again. Our job was done.

A few days later Jenny called me at work. "I just got off the phone with Colleen McGarr," she said. "You are *not* going to believe it."

"Go on," I said.

"She says the director wants Marley to try out," Jenny said.

"Marley?" I asked, certain I had misheard. She didn't seem to notice the surprise in my voice.

"Apparently, he's looking for a big, dumb, loopy dog to play the role of the family pet," she explained. "Marley caught his eye."

"Loopy?" I asked.

"That's what Colleen says he wants. Big, dumb, and loopy."

Well, he had certainly come to the right place.

Colleen picked up Marley the next day. Knowing the importance of a good entrance, he came racing through the living room to greet her at full speed, pausing only long enough to grab the nearest pillow in his teeth. (You never knew when a busy film director might need a quick nap, and if he did, I guess Marley wanted to be ready.)

When he hit the wood floor, he flew into a full skid. He didn't stop until he hit the coffee table, went airborne, crashed into a chair, landed on his back, rolled, scrambled back to his feet, and collided head-on into Colleen's legs.

At least he didn't jump up, I noted.

Colleen drove off in her red pickup truck with our desperately happy dog beside her.

Two hours later Colleen and Company were back. The verdict was in—Marley had passed the audition.

"Oh, shut up!" Jenny shrieked. "No way!"

I asked her how the audition went.

"I got Marley in the car and it was like driving in a Jacuzzi," she said. "He was slobbering on everything. By the time I got him there, I was drenched."

They arrived at production headquarters at the Gulf Stream Hotel a few miles from our house. Marley immediately impressed the crew by jumping out of the truck and tearing around the parking lot in random patterns. He moved like he expected bombs to start dropping at any moment.

"He was just berserk, completely mental," Colleen recounted.

"Yeah, he gets a little excited," I said.

"At one point, Marley grabbed the checkbook out of a crew member's hand and raced away," she explained.

"He ran around in a bunch of tight figure eights to nowhere."

"We call him our Labrador evader," Jenny apologized. Then she made the kind of smile only a proud mother can make.

Marley eventually calmed down enough to convince everyone he could do the part, which was basically to just play himself. The movie was called *The Last Home Run*. In it, a seventy-nine-year-old man becomes a twelve-year-old for five days to live his dream of playing Little League ball. Marley was cast as the hyperactive family dog of the Little League coach, played by retired major-league catcher Gary Carter.

"They really want him to be in their movie?" I asked.

"Everyone loved him," Colleen said. "He's perfect." She explained that we wouldn't get paid, but I didn't care. My dog was going to be a star!

In the days leading up to shooting, we noticed a change in Marley's behavior. A strange calm had come over him. It was as if passing the audition had given him new confidence. He was almost regal.

"Maybe he just needed someone to believe in him," I told Jenny.

If anyone believed, it was Jenny, Stage Mom Extraordinaire. As the first day of filming approached, she bathed him. She brushed him. She clipped his nails and swabbed out his ears.

On the morning shooting was to begin, I walked out of the bedroom to find Jenny and Marley tangled together. They seemed to be locked in mortal combat, bouncing across the room. She was straddling him like a horse, with her knees tightly hugging his ribs. One hand grasped the end of his choke chain as he bucked and lurched. It was like having a rodeo right in my own living room.

"What on earth are you doing?" I asked.

"What's it look like?" she shot back. "Brushing his teeth!"

Sure enough, Jenny had a toothbrush in the other hand and was doing her best to scrub his big white ivories. Frothing at the mouth, Marley did his best to eat the toothbrush. He looked positively rabid.

"Are you using toothpaste?" I asked.

"Baking soda," she answered.

"Thank goodness," I said. "So it's *not* rabies?"

An hour later, we left for the Gulf Stream Hotel. The boys sat in their car seats with Marley between them, panting away with abnormally fresh breath. Colleen had told us to arrive by 9:00 A.M., but a block away, traffic came to a standstill. Up ahead, the road was barricaded and a police officer was diverting traffic away from the hotel. The movie was the biggest event to hit the town in fifteen years, and a crowd of spectators had turned out to gawk. The police were keeping everyone away.

We inched forward in traffic. When we finally got up to the officer, I leaned out the window and said, "We need to get through."

"No one gets through," he said. "Keep moving. Let's go."

"We're with the cast," I said.

The officer eyed us skeptically—a couple in a minivan with two toddlers and the family pet. "I said move it!" he barked.

"Our dog is in the film," I said.

Suddenly he looked at me with new respect. "You have the dog?" he asked. The dog was on his checklist.

"I have the dog," I said. "Marley the Dog."

"Playing himself," Jenny chimed in.

He turned around and blew his whistle with great fanfare. "He's got the dog!" he shouted to a cop a half block down. "Marley the Dog!"

And that cop yelled to someone else, "He's got the dog! Marley the Dog's here!"

"Let 'em through!" a third officer shouted from the distance.

"Let 'em through!" the second cop echoed.

The officer moved the barricade and waved us through. "Right this way," he said politely. I felt like royalty. As we rolled past him he said once again, as if he could not quite believe it, "He's got the dog."

In the parking lot outside the hotel, the film crew was ready for action. Cables crisscrossed the pavement. Camera tripods and microphone booms were set up. Lights hung from scaffolding. Trailers held racks of costumes. Two large tables of food and drinks were set up in the shade for cast and crew. Important-looking people in sunglasses bustled about.

The director greeted us and gave us a quick rundown of Marley's scene. It went like this: A minivan pulls up to the curb. Marley's make-believe owner is at the wheel. Her daughter and son are in the back with their family dog, played by Marley. The daughter opens the sliding door and hops out. Her brother follows with Marley on a leash. They walk off camera. End of scene.

"Easy enough," I told the director. "He should be able to handle that, no problem." I pulled Marley off to the side to wait for his cue to get into the van.

"Okay, people, listen up," the director told the crew. "The dog's a little nutty, okay? But unless he completely hijacks the scene, we're going to keep rolling. Just let him do his thing," he coached, "and work around him."

When everyone was set to go, I loaded Marley into the van and handed his nylon leash to the little boy, who looked terrified. "He's friendly," I told him. "He'll just want to lick you. See?" I stuck my wrist in Marley's mouth to demonstrate.

When filming started, the scene turned out to be a little trickier than I'd expected. The reason was simple—Marley.

Take one. The van pulls to the curb. The daughter slides open the side door. A yellow streak shoots out. Like a giant furball being fired from a cannon, it blurs past the cameras.

"Cut!" the director shouted.

I chased Marley down in the parking lot and hauled him back.

"Okay, folks, we're going to try that again," the director said. Then, to the boy, he coached gently, "The dog's pretty wild. Try to hold on tighter this time."

Take two. The van pulls to the curb. The door slides open. The daughter is just beginning to exit when Marley huffs into view and leaps out past her. This time he drags the white-knuckled and white-faced boy behind him.

"Cut!" the director shouted.

Take three. The van pulls up. The door slides open. The daughter exits. The boy exits, holding the leash. As he steps away from the van the leash pulls taut, but no dog follows. The boy begins to tug, heave, and pull. He leans into it and gives it everything he has. Not a budge. Long, painful seconds pass. The boy grimaces and looks back at the camera.

"Cut!" the director shouted.

I peered into the van to find Marley bent over, licking himself. He looked up at me as if to say, "Can't you see I'm busy?"

Take four. I load Marley into the back of the van with the boy and shut the door. The van pulls to the curb. The door slides open. The daughter steps out. The boy steps out—with a bewildered look on his face. He peers directly into the camera and holds up his hand. Dangling from it is half the leash. The end is jagged and wet with saliva.

"Cut! Cut! Cut!" the director shouted.

The boy explained that as he waited in the van, Marley began gnawing on the leash and wouldn't stop. The crew and cast were staring at the severed leash in disbelief. A mix of awe and horror formed on their faces. It was like nothing they'd ever seen. I, on the other hand, was not surprised in the least. Marley had destroyed more leashes and ropes than I could remember.

"Okay, everybody, let's take a break," the director called out. He turned to me and asked in an amazingly calm voice, "How quickly can you find a new leash?" I knew that every minute cost big money.

"There's a pet store a half mile from here," I said. "I can be back in fifteen minutes."

"And this time get something he can't chew through," he said.

I returned with a heavy chain leash that looked like something a lion trainer might use. The filming continued, but each scene was worse than the one before. At one point, the actress who played the daughter let out a desperate shriek midscene and screamed with true horror in her voice, "Oh, no! His thing is out!"

"Cut!" the director shouted.

That's how Day One of shooting went. Marley was

a disaster—a complete and total disaster. Part of me was defensive. *Well, what did they expect for free? Benji?* Part of me was mortified. I glanced at the cast and crew. The looks on their faces screamed, "Where did this animal come from, and how can we send him back?"

"Don't bother coming in tomorrow," one of the assistants told us at the end of the day. "We'll call if we need Marley." To make sure there was no confusion, he repeated, "So unless you hear from us, don't show up. Got it?"

Yeah, I got it, loud and clear. The director had sent his assistant to do the dirty work.

Marley's acting career was over. Not that I could blame them. Marley had been a nightmare. Thanks to him, thousands of dollars had been wasted. He had slimed countless costumes, raided the snack table, and nearly knocked over a $30,000 camera. It was the old "don't call us, we'll call you" routine.

"Marley," I said when we got home, "your big chance and you really blew it."

11

Take Two

The next morning the phone rang. It was the assistant, telling us to get Marley to the hotel as soon as possible.

"You mean you want him back?" I asked.

"Right away," he said. "The director wants him in the next scene."

I arrived thirty minutes later, still not quite believing they had invited us back. The director was all fired up. He had watched the raw footage from the day before and could not have been happier.

"The dog was hysterical!" he gushed. "Just hilarious. Pure madcap genius!" I could feel myself standing taller, chest puffing out.

"We always knew he was a natural," Jenny said.

Shooting continued for several more days, and Marley continued to rise to the occasion. He was lapping up stardom. The crew, especially the women, fawned over him. The weather was brutally hot, and one assistant had to follow Marley around with a bowl and a bottle of spring water, pouring him drinks whenever he wanted. Everyone, it seemed, was feeding him snacks off the buffet table.

I left him with the crew for a couple hours while I checked in at work. When I returned, I found him sprawled out like King Tut, paws in the air, accepting a leisurely belly rub from the makeup artist. "He's such a lover!" she cooed.

Stardom was starting to go to my head, too. I began introducing myself as "Marley the Dog's handler." I dropped lines such as, "For his next movie, we're hoping for a barking part."

During one break in the shooting, I walked into the hotel lobby to use the pay phone. Marley was off his leash and sniffing around the furniture several feet away. A concierge, apparently mistaking my star for a stray, tried to hustle him out a side door.

"Go home!" he scolded. "Shoo!"

"Excuse me?" I said, cupping my hand over the mouthpiece of the phone and shooting him my most withering stare. "Do you have any idea who you're talking to?"

We remained on the set for four straight days. But it was two full years later before I finally got my chance to see Marley's acting skills.

I was in Blockbuster when on a whim I asked the clerk if he knew anything about a movie called *The Last Home Run*. He knew about it *and* he had it in stock. In fact, as luck would have it, not a single copy was checked out.

I raced home with a copy and yelled to Jenny and the kids to gather around the VCR. Marley was on screen for less than two minutes. But they were definitely two of the livelier minutes in the film. We laughed! We cried! We cheered!

"Waddy, that you!" Conor screamed.

"We're famous!" Patrick yelled.

Marley yawned and crawled under the coffee table. By the end of the movie, he was sound asleep. We held our breath and waited to see his name in the credits. For a while, I thought they were going to leave him out. But then there it was, listed in big letters across the screen for all to see.

MARLEY THE DOG . . . AS HIMSELF.

12

Jail Break

One month after filming ended for *The Last Home Run*, we said good-bye to our home in West Palm Beach and all the memories it held. We needed more room for our growing family, and we moved into a new house in Boca Raton.

From our living-room window we could see a small city park filled with playground equipment. The kids adored it. And our new house had an inground swimming pool.

No one loved the pool more than our water dog. If

the pool gate was open, Marley would charge for the water. Getting a running start from the family room, he flew out the open doors. With one bounce off the brick patio, he'd land in the pool on his belly with a giant flop that sent a geyser into the air and waves over the edge.

Swimming with Marley was potentially life threatening, a little like swimming with an ocean liner. He would come at you full speed ahead, his paws flailing out in front of him. You'd expect him to veer away at the last minute, but he would simply crash into you and try to climb aboard. If you were over your head, he could push you beneath the surface.

"What do I look like, a dock?" I would say, and cradle him in my arms to let him catch his breath. His front paws paddled away on autopilot as he licked the water off my face.

One thing our new house did not have was a Marley-proof bunker. At our old house, the concrete one-car garage was pretty much indestructible, and it had two windows that kept it comfortable even in the dead of summer. Our Boca house had a two-car garage, but it had no windows and was stiflingly hot. Sometimes the temperature felt like 150 degrees. We needed to find a place for him in the house.

The first time we left him alone in our new house, we shut him in the laundry room, just off the kitchen, with a blanket and a big bowl of water. When we returned a few hours later, he had scratched up the door. The damage was minor, but we knew it was a bad sign, considering his horrible fear of thunder.

"Maybe he's just getting used to his new surroundings," I offered.

"There's not even a cloud in the sky," Jenny observed skeptically. "What's going to happen the first time a storm hits?"

The next time we left him alone, we found out. As thunderheads rolled in, we cut our outing short and hurried home. It was too late. Jenny was a few steps ahead of me. She opened the laundry-room door.

"Oh my goodness." She said it the way you would if you had just entered a crime scene. Again: "Oh . . . my . . . goodness."

I peeked in over her shoulder, and it was worse than I had feared. Marley was standing there, panting frantically, his paws and mouth bleeding. Loose fur was everywhere, as though the thunder had scared the hair right out of his coat. The damage was worse than anything he had ever done before, and that was saying a lot.

An entire wall was gouged open. Plaster and wood chips and bent nails were everywhere. Electric wiring lay exposed. Blood smeared the floor and the walls.

"Oh my goodness," Jenny said a third time.

"Oh my goodness," I repeated. It was all either of us could say.

"Okay, we can handle this. It's all fixable," I said, after several seconds of just standing there mute.

"A few hundred bucks and we'll be good as new," she chirped.

"That's what I'm thinking, too," I said.

As we talked, Marley curled up on the rug in front of the kitchen sink and let out a deep sigh. I knelt beside him and stroked his blood-caked fur. "Geez, dog," I said. "What are we going to do with you?" Without lifting his head, he looked up at me with the saddest, most mournful eyes I have ever seen, and just gazed at me. It was as if he were trying to tell me something, something important he needed me to understand.

"I know," I said. "I know you can't help it."

The next day Jenny and I took the boys with us to the pet store and bought a giant steel cage. They came in all different sizes for all different size dogs. When I described Marley to the clerk, he led us to the largest one of all. It was enormous and made out of heavy steel with two locks to hold the door securely shut. It was big enough for a lion to stand up and turn around in and had a heavy steel pan for a floor. This was our answer, our own portable prison.

Conor and Patrick both crawled inside and I slid the bolts shut, locking them in for a moment. "What do you guys think?" I asked. "Will this hold our super dog?"

Conor teetered at the cage door, his fingers through the bars, and said, "Me in jail."

"Waddy's going to be our prisoner!" Patrick chimed in, delighted at the prospect.

Back home, we set up the crate next to the washing machine. The cage took up nearly half the laundry room. "Come here, Marley!" I called when it was fully assembled. I tossed a Milk-Bone in and he happily pranced in after it. I closed and bolted the door behind him, and he stood there chewing his treat, unfazed by the new life experience he was about to enter, the one known in prison as "solitary confinement."

"This is going to be your new home when we're

away," I said cheerfully. Marley stood there panting contentedly, not a trace of concern on his face, and then he lay down and let out a sigh. "A good sign," I said to Jenny. "A very good sign."

That evening we decided to give the maximum-security dog jail cell a test run. This time I didn't even need a Milk-Bone to lure Marley in. I simply opened the gate, gave a whistle, and in he walked, tail banging the metal sides.

"Be a good boy, Marley," I said.

"You know something?" Jenny said as we loaded the boys in the minivan to go out to dinner.

"What?" I asked.

"This is the first time since we got him that I don't have a knot in my stomach leaving Marley alone in the house," she said. "I never even realized how much it put me on edge until now."

"I know what you mean," I said. "It was always a guessing game: 'What will our dog destroy this time?'"

"I think that crate is going to be the best money we ever spent," she said.

"We should have done this a long time ago," I agreed. "You can't put a price on peace of mind."

We had a great dinner out, followed by a sunset

stroll on the beach. The boys splashed in the surf, chased seagulls, and threw fistfuls of sand into the water.

"What a nice outing this has been," Jenny said as we walked up the front sidewalk to our house.

I was about to agree with her when I noticed something out of the corner of my eye—something up ahead that was not quite right. I turned my head and stared at the window beside the front door. The miniblinds were shut, as they always were when we left the house. But about a foot up from the bottom of the window, the metal slats were bent apart and something was sticking through them.

Something black. And wet. And pressed up against the glass.

"What the. . . ?" I said. "How could. . . ? Marley?"

When I opened the front door, sure enough, there was our one-dog welcoming committee, wiggling all over the foyer, pleased as punch to have us home again. We checked every room and closet for signs of Marley's unsupervised adventure. Amazingly, the house was fine. We converged on the laundry room. The crate's door stood wide open. It was as if some secret accomplice had snuck in and sprung our inmate.

I squatted beside the cage to have a closer look. The

two locks were both slid back into the open position, and they were dripping with saliva.

"It looks like an inside job," I said. "Somehow Houdini here licked his way out."

"I can't believe it," Jenny said.

We always fancied Marley to be as dumb as algae, but he had been clever enough to figure out how to stick his long, strong tongue through the bars to slowly work the barrels free from their slots. He had licked his way to freedom. He proved over the coming weeks that he was able to repeat the trick easily whenever he wanted. Some days we would return to find him resting peacefully in the cage, other days to find him waiting at the front window.

We took to wiring both locks in place with heavy electrical cable. That worked for a while. But one day, with distant thunder rumbling on the horizon, we came home to find that the bottom corner of the cage's gate had been peeled back. It looked as though someone had used a giant can opener. Panicky Marley was firmly stuck around the rib cage, half in and half out of the tight opening. I bent the steel gate back into place as best I could, and we began wiring all four corners of the door, as well as the locks. Pretty soon we were reinforcing the corners of the cage itself as Marley continued to put his brawn into busting out.

Within three months, the gleaming steel cage we had thought was Marley-proof looked like it had taken a direct hit from a cannon. The bars were twisted and bent and the frame pried apart. The door hardly fit anymore, and the sides bulged outward. I continued to reinforce it as best I could, and it continued to hold tenuously against Marley's full-bodied assaults. Whatever false sense of security the contraption had once offered us was gone. Each time we left, even for a half hour, we wondered whether this would be the time that our manic inmate would bust out. When would he go on another couch-shredding, wall-gouging, door-eating rampage?

So much for peace of mind.

13

Dinnertime!

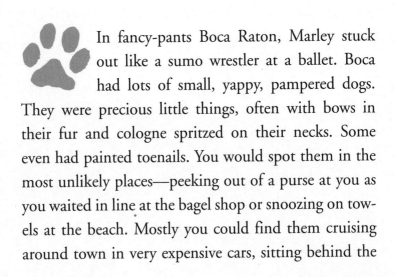 In fancy-pants Boca Raton, Marley stuck out like a sumo wrestler at a ballet. Boca had lots of small, yappy, pampered dogs. They were precious little things, often with bows in their fur and cologne spritzed on their necks. Some even had painted toenails. You would spot them in the most unlikely places—peeking out of a purse at you as you waited in line at the bagel shop or snoozing on towels at the beach. Mostly you could find them cruising around town in very expensive cars, sitting behind the

steering wheels on their owners' laps. They were petite and sophisticated. Marley was big and clunky. He *really* wanted to hang out with the popular pooches. They wanted nothing to do with him.

Thanks to obedience school, Marley was fairly manageable on walks. But if he saw something he liked, he still wouldn't hesitate to lunge for it. He didn't care if he choked himself in the process.

Each time he spotted one of the pampered pups around town, he would break into a gallop, dragging Jenny or me behind him at the end of the leash. The choke chain would tighten around his throat, making him gasp and cough. Each time Marley would be snubbed—not only by the Boca minidog but by the Boca minidog's owner, *too*. The owner would snatch up young Fifi or Suzi or Cheri as if rescuing her from the jaws of an alligator. Marley did not seem to mind. When the next minidog came into sight, he would do it all over again.

One Sunday afternoon, Jenny and I thought it would be fun to take the whole family for an outside meal at one of the popular restaurants. We loaded the boys into the minivan. Even Marley came. In Boca, it was a tradition for dogs to eat at their owners' feet.

We found a restaurant with outside tables, and I hooked the end of Marley's leash to one of the legs. We ordered drinks all around.

"To a beautiful day with my beautiful family," Jenny said, holding up her glass for a toast. We clicked our glasses, and the boys smashed their sippy cups into each other.

That's when it happened. It happened so fast, in fact, that we didn't even realize it had happened. All we knew was that our table started moving. It was crashing its way through the sea of other tables.

Banging into innocent bystanders and making a horrible, ear-piercing, industrial-grade shriek, it scraped over the concrete sidewalk. What was going on? Was our table under a spell? I quickly saw that it wasn't our table that was haunted, but our dog. Marley was out in front, chugging forward with every ounce of rippling muscle he had.

In the fraction of a second after that, I saw just where Marley was heading. Fifty feet down the sidewalk, a delicate French poodle lingered at her owner's side, nose in the air.

Jenny and I both sat there for a moment longer, drinks in hand, the boys between us in their stroller. We wanted our perfect little Sunday afternoon to last. There was just one problem—our table was now motoring its way through the crowd. An instant later, we were on our feet, screaming and running.

"Sorry!" we said to the customers around us. "Really really sorry."

I was the first to reach the runaway table. I grabbed on, planted my feet, and leaned back with everything I had. Soon Jenny was beside me, pulling back too. I felt like we were action heroes in a Western movie, giving our all to rein in the runaway train before it jumped the tracks and plunged over a cliff.

When we finally got the table stopped and Marley reeled in, just feet from the poodle and her mortified owner, I turned back to check on the boys. That's when I got my first good look at the faces of my fellow diners. Men stopped in midconversation, cell phones in their hands. Women stared with opened mouths.

It was finally Conor who broke the silence. "Waddy go walk!" he screamed with delight.

A waiter rushed up and helped me drag the table back into place as Jenny held Marley in a death grip. He still hadn't taken his eyes off the poodle. "Let me get some new place settings," the waiter said.

"That won't be necessary," Jenny said nonchalantly. "We'll just pay for our drinks and go."

Soon after our outdoor dining fiasco, I found a book in the library titled *No Bad Dogs* by Barbara Woodhouse. The author believed that if a dog misbehaved, it wasn't the dog's problem. It was a problem with the people who hadn't trained him very well. The book described some of the worst canine behaviors imaginable.

There were dogs that howled nonstop, dug nonstop, fought nonstop, and bit nonstop. There were dogs that hated all men and dogs that hated all women. Dogs that stole from their masters and dogs that jealously attacked defenseless infants. There were even dogs that ate their own poop. *Thank God,* I thought, *at least he doesn't eat his own poop.*

Not long after I read Woodhouse's book, a neighbor asked us to take in their cat for a week while they were on vacation.

"Sure," we said. "Bring him over." Compared to a dog, cats were easy. Cats ran on autopilot. This cat was shy and elusive, especially around Marley. He hid under the couch all day and came out to eat his food and use the kitty litter box when we were asleep. We kept the food high out of Marley's reach and tucked the litter box away in a corner of the patio. There was nothing to it, really. Marley seemed totally unaware the cat was even in the house.

Midway through the cat's stay with us, I awoke at dawn to a loud, driving beat traveling through the mattress. It was Marley, quivering with excitement beside the bed, his tail slapping the mattress at a furious rate. *Whomp! Whomp! Whomp!* I reached out to pet him. He began prancing and dancing beside the bed. The Marley Mambo.

"Okay, what do you have?" I asked him, eyes still shut. As if to answer, Marley proudly plopped his prize onto the crisp sheets, just inches from my face. In my groggy state, it took me a minute to process what exactly it was. The object was small, dark, and coated in a coarse, gritty sand. Then the smell reached my nostrils. An acrid, pungent, putrid smell. I bolted upright and pushed backward against Jenny, waking her up. I pointed at Marley's gift to us, glistening on the sheets.

"That's not. . . ," Jenny began, disgust in her voice.

"Yes, it is," I said. "He raided the kitty litter box."

Marley could not have looked more pleased had he just presented us with the Hope Diamond. As Barbara Woodhouse had predicted, our mentally unstable, abnormal mutt had entered the poop-eating stage of his life.

14

Lightning Strikes

 On January 9, 1997, Jenny gave me a belated Christmas present: a pink-cheeked, seven-pound baby girl. We named her Colleen.

When Colleen was one week old, Jenny brought her outside for the first time. The day was crisp and beautiful, and the boys and I were in the front yard, planting flowers. Marley was chained to a tree nearby, happy to lie in the shade and watch the world go by.

Jenny sat in the grass beside Marley and put Colleen in a portable bassinette on the ground between them.

After several minutes, the boys called for Mom to come closer to see what they had planted. They led Jenny and me around the garden beds as Colleen napped in the shade beside Marley. We wandered behind some large shrubbery. We could still see the baby, but from the street no one could see us.

An older couple walking by had stopped and were gawking at the scene in our front yard with bewildered expressions. We peeked at them through the shrubs. At first I was not sure what had made them stop and stare. Then it hit me: All they could see was a fragile newborn alone with a large yellow dog, who appeared to be baby-sitting single-handedly. They had no idea we were right there.

There was Marley, looking like an Egyptian sphinx, lying with his front paws crossed, head up, panting contentedly. Every few seconds he sniffed the baby's head. Then Marley rested his chin across the baby's stomach, his head bigger than her whole body, and let out a long sigh. It was as if he were saying, "When are those two going to get home?" It looked like he was protecting her, and maybe he was, but I'm pretty sure he was just trying to get a whiff of her diaper.

Jenny and I stood there in the bushes and exchanged

grins. The thought of Marley as doggie day care was just too good to let go. I was tempted to wait there and see how the scene would play out, but I was afraid the couple might call 911. We stepped out of the bushes and waved to the couple, who looked relieved to see us.

"You must really trust your dog," the woman said.

"He hasn't eaten one yet," I said.

When Marley was about six years old, his intense fear of thunder finally made sense. I was in the backyard on a Sunday afternoon. The skies grew darker as I dug up a rectangle of grass to plant a vegetable garden. Marley paced nervously around me. His internal barometer told him a storm was coming. I sensed it, too, but I wanted to get the project done. I figured I would work until I felt the first drops of rain. As I dug, I kept glancing at the sky, watching an ominous black thunderhead far away, out over the ocean. Marley was whining softly, beckoning me to put down the shovel and head inside.

"Relax," I told him. "It's still miles away."

The words had barely left my lips when I felt a kind of quivering tingle on the back of my neck. The sky had turned an odd shade of olive-gray. The air went dead, as though some heavenly force had grabbed the winds and frozen them in its grip.

Weird, I thought as I leaned on my shovel to study the sky. That's when I heard it—a buzzing, popping, crackling surge of energy. *Pfffffffffft.* The sound filled the air around me. Then silence. I knew trouble was coming, but I had no time to react. In the next fraction of a second, the sky went pure, blindingly white. An explosion boomed in my ears. I had never heard anything like it before—not in any storm, at any fireworks display, or at any demolition site. A wall of energy hit me in the chest like an invisible linebacker.

I don't know how many seconds later I opened my eyes. I was lying facedown on the ground with sand in my mouth. Marley was down, too—in his hit-the-deck stance. When he saw me raise my head, he wiggled toward me on his belly like a soldier trying to slide beneath barbed wire. Reaching me, he climbed right on my back and buried his snout in my neck, frantically licking me.

"Come on!" I yelled. Marley and I were on our feet, sprinting through the downpour toward the back door as new bolts of lightning flashed around us. We did not stop until we were safely inside. I knelt on the floor, soaking wet, catching my breath. Marley clambered all over me, licking my face, nibbling my ears, flinging spit and loose fur all over everything. He was beside himself with fear, shaking uncontrollably, drool hanging off his chin. I hugged him and tried to calm him down.

"That was close!" I said, and realized that I was shaking, too.

Marley looked up at me with those big eyes that I swore could almost talk. I was sure I knew what he was trying to tell me. "I've been trying to warn you for years that this stuff can kill you. But would anyone listen? Now will you take me seriously?"

The dog had a point.

Maybe his fear of thunder had not been so crazy after all. I pulled Marley into my lap, all ninety-seven nervous pounds of him, and made him a promise right then and there: Never again would I dismiss his fear of this deadly force of nature.

15

Dog Beach

On a drop-dead-perfect June morning, Marley and I headed for Dog Beach.

Dog Beach was one of the last stretches of ocean sand in Florida where dogs and their owners could play. The rules were simple: Aggressive dogs had to stay leashed. All others could run free. Owners were to bring plastic bags with them to pick up any poop. All trash, including bagged dog waste, was to be carted out. Each dog was supposed to arrive with a supply of fresh drinking water.

But the most important rule: No pooping in the water.

I filled the car with as many beach towels as I could find—and that was just for the drive over. As always, Marley's tongue was hanging out, spit flying everywhere. I felt like I was on a road trip with Old Faithful. My only regret was that the windshield wipers were not on the inside.

I parked the car and began the long hike to the beach. Marley led the charge. Just as we reached the path to the water, Marley squatted in the weeds and laid a giant log. Perfect. At least that was out of the way. I bagged it up.

"To the beach!" I commanded.

As we came up over the top of the sand dune, I was surprised to see several people wading in the shallow water with their dogs on leashes. I expected the dogs to be romping and playing together off their leashes.

"What's going on?" I wondered out loud.

"A sheriff's deputy was just here," one glum dog owner explained to me. "He said from now on they're enforcing the county leash law. We'll be fined if our dogs are loose."

I was too late. The police were tightening the noose. I obediently walked Marley along the water's edge with the other dog owners. It felt more like prison than paradise.

I returned with Marley to my towel and poured him a bowl of water from the canteen. A shirtless, tattooed man in cutoff blue jeans and work boots came over the dune leading a muscular and fierce-looking pit bull terrier on a heavy chain.

The owner must have seen my fear. "Don't you worry," he called out. "Killer's friendly. He don't never fight other dogs." I was just beginning to exhale with relief when he added, "But you should see him rip open a wild hog! I'll tell you, he can get it down and gutted in about fifteen seconds."

Marley and Killer the Pig-Slaying Pit Bull strained at their leashes, circling, sniffing furiously at each other. Marley had never been in a fight in his life. He was so much bigger than most other dogs that he had never been intimidated by a challenge, either. Even when a dog attempted to pick a fight, he didn't take the hint. He would pounce into a playful stance, butt up, tail wagging, a dumb, happy grin on his face. But he had never before been confronted by a trained killer. I pictured

Killer lunging without warning for Marley's throat and not letting go.

But Killer's owner wasn't concerned. "Unless you're a wild hog, he'll just lick you to death," he said.

I told him the cops had just been here and were going to ticket people who did not obey the leash law. "I guess they're cracking down," I said.

The man yelled and spit into the sand. "I've been bringing my dogs to this beach for years. You don't need no leash at Dog Beach!" He unclipped the heavy chain, and Killer galloped across the sand and into the water. Marley reared back on his hind legs, bouncing up and down. He looked at Killer and then up at me. He looked back at Killer and back at me. His paws padded nervously on the sand and he let out a soft whimper. I looked around. No police were anywhere in sight. I looked at Marley. If he could've talked, I knew he would say, "Please! Please! Pretty please! I'll be good. I promise."

"Go ahead, let him loose," Killer's owner said. "A dog ain't meant to spend his life on the end of a rope."

"Oh, what the heck," I said, and unsnapped the leash. Marley dashed for the water, kicking sand all over us as he blasted off. He crashed into the surf just as a breaker rolled in, tossing him under water. A second later his head reappeared. The instant he got back on his feet, he threw a cross-body block at Killer the Pig-Slaying Pit Bull. They both went down into water. Together they rolled beneath a wave. When they popped back up again, their tails were wagging, their mouths grinning. Killer jumped onto Marley's back and Marley onto Killer's, their jaws clamping playfully around each other's throats. They chased each other up the waterline and back again, sending plumes of spray flying on either side of them. They pranced, they danced, they wrestled, they dove. I don't think I had ever before or have ever since seen such pure joy.

Pretty soon all the dogs on the beach were running free. The twelve or so dogs all got along incredibly well. The owners all followed the rules. It was Dog Beach as it was meant to be.

There was only one small problem. As the morning went on, Marley kept lapping up saltwater. I followed behind him with the bowl of fresh water, but he was too distracted to drink. Several times I led him right up to the bowl and stuck his nose into it, but he rejected the fresh water as if it were vinegar.

Out in the shallow water, he paused from his play to lap up even more saltwater. "Stop that, you dummy," I yelled at him. "You're going to make yourself—"

Before I could finish my thought, it happened. A strange glaze settled over his eyes. A horrible churning sound began to erupt from his gut. He arched his back high and opened and shut his mouth several times, as if trying to clear something from his craw. His shoulders heaved. His abdomen contorted.

I hurried to finish my sentence. "—sick."

The same instant that word left my lips, Marley committed the ultimate Dog Beach no-no.

"*GAAAAAAAAACK!*" Marley let out a big barfing sound.

I raced to pull him out of the water, but it was too late. Everything was coming up.

"*GAAAAAAAAACK!*" I could see last night's dog chow floating on the water's surface. I could see undigested corn kernels that he had swiped off the kids' plates bobbing among the nuggets. A milk-jug cap and the severed head of a tiny plastic soldier also appeared.

The whole embarrassing episode took fewer than three seconds. The instant his stomach was emptied, he looked up brightly, as if to say, "Now that I've got that taken care of, who wants to body surf?"

I glanced nervously around me, but no one had

seemed to notice. The other dog owners were occupied with their own dogs, farther down the beach. Nearby, a mother helped her toddler make a sand castle. The sunbathers were lying flat on their backs, eyes closed.

Thank goodness! I thought. I waded into Marley's puke zone, stirring the water with my feet to hide the evidence. *How embarrassing would that have been?* Maybe we had broken the No. 1 Dog Beach Rule, but we hadn't caused any real harm. After all, it was just undigested food. The fish would be thankful for the meal. Wouldn't they? I even picked out the milk-jug cap and soldier's head and put them in my pocket. I didn't want to litter.

"Listen, you," I said sternly, grabbing Marley around the snout and forcing him to look me in the eye. "Stop drinking saltwater. What kind of a dog doesn't know enough to not drink saltwater?" I thought about yanking him off the beach and cutting our adventure short, but now he seemed fine. There couldn't possibly be anything left in his stomach. The damage was done, and we had gotten away with it. I released him, and he streaked down the beach to play with Killer.

But there was something I hadn't thought of. Marley's stomach may have been completely emptied, but his bowels were not. The sun was reflecting blindingly off the water. I squinted to see Marley frolicking among the other dogs. As I watched, he stopped playing and began turning in tight circles in the shallow water. I knew what that meant. It was what he did every morning in the backyard after breakfast. Sometimes the circling could go on for a minute or more as he sought just the perfect patch of earth on which to relieve himself. And now he was circling in the shallows of Dog Beach— where no dog had dared to poop before. *Oh, no!*

When he finished circling, Marley squatted. And this time, he had an audience. Killer's dad and several other dog owners were standing just a few yards from him. The mother and her daughter had turned from their sand castle to gaze out to sea. A couple holding hands walked along the water's edge.

"No," I whispered to Marley—even though he couldn't hear. "Please, no."

"Hey!" someone yelled out. "Get your dog!"

"Stop him!" someone else shouted.

As alarmed voices cried out, the sunbathers sat up to see what all the commotion was about.

I burst into a full sprint. I had to get to him before it was too late. If I could just reach him and yank him out of his squat before he let loose, I might be able to stop him. Each step seemed to last forever. Each foot hit the sand with a dull thud. My arms swung through the air. My face scrunched in a sort of agonized grimace.

I felt as if I were moving in slow motion. So was everything around me. A young woman sunbather plastered her hand over her mouth. The mother scooped up her child and retreated from the water's edge. The dog owners, their faces twisted with disgust, pointed. Killer's dad, his leathery neck bulging, yelled. Marley was done circling now and in full squat position, looking up to the heavens as if saying a little prayer.

"Noooooooooooooooo!" I screamed. I was almost there, just feet from him. "Marley, no! No, Marley, No! No! No! No!" It was no use. Just as I reached him, he exploded in a burst of watery diarrhea. Everyone was jumping back now, fleeing to higher ground. Owners grabbed their dogs. Sunbathers scooped up their towels.

Then it was over. Marley trotted out of the water onto the beach, shook off, and turned to look at me, panting happily. I pulled a plastic bag out of my pocket and held it helplessly in the air. It was useless. The waves crashed in and spread Marley's mess across the water and up onto the beach.

"Dude," Killer's dad said. "That was not cool."

No, it wasn't cool at all. Marley and I had violated the most important rule of Dog Beach. We had vomited and pooped in the water—and ruined the morning for everyone. It was time to leave. Quickly.

"Sorry," I mumbled to Killer's owner as I snapped the leash on Marley. "He swallowed a bunch of sea-water."

Back at the car, I threw a towel over Marley and vigorously rubbed him down. The more I rubbed, the more he shook. Soon I was covered in sand and spray and fur. I wanted to be mad at him. I wanted to strangle him.

But it was too late now. Besides, Marley hadn't meant to do it. He hadn't disobeyed a command or purposely tried to humiliate me. He simply had to go, and he went. It just happened to be at the wrong place and wrong time and in front of all the wrong people. I could have killed him, except I knew he was a victim of his own tiny brain. He was the only beast on the whole beach dumb enough to guzzle seawater. How could I hold that against him?

"You don't have to look so pleased with yourself," I said as I loaded him into the backseat. But pleased he was. He could not have looked happier had I bought him his own Caribbean island. What he did not know was that this would be his last time setting a paw in any body of saltwater. His days as a beach bum were over.

16

A Northbound Plane

In 1999 we packed up our house and left Florida. I had gotten a new job in Pennsylvania. On moving day, we arrived at the airport with two frogs, three goldfish, a hermit crab, a snail named Sluggy, and a box of live crickets for feeding the frogs.

And, of course, Marley. Like most things that involved Marley, getting him on the plane wasn't easy. He had to ride in a crate where the luggage was stored.

We stepped up to the airline counter with Marley on

his leash. A woman in uniform looked at Marley, then looked at the crate I had brought for him. "We can't allow that dog aboard in that container," she said. "He's too big for it."

"The pet store said this was the 'large dog' size," I pleaded. (I hadn't actually checked to make sure our *very* large dog would fit.)

"Airline rules say that the dog has to be able to stand up and turn all the way around," she explained. "Go ahead. Give it a try."

I opened the gate and called Marley. He was not about to walk voluntarily into jail. I pushed him and prodded him. He didn't budge.

I searched my pockets for something to bribe him with. Where were the dog biscuits when I needed them? I found a tin of breath mints.

This is as good as it's going to get, I thought. I took one out and held it in front of his nose. "Want a mint, Marley? Go get the mint!" and I tossed it into the crate. Sure enough, he took the bait and walked right into the box.

The lady was right. He didn't quite fit. He scrunched down so his head wouldn't hit the ceiling. His butt stuck out the open door.

I scrunched his tail down and closed the gate, shoving his rear inside. "See?" I said. "He fits."

"He's got to be able to turn around," the woman told me.

"Turn around, boy," I called, giving a little whistle. "Come on, turn around."

Marley shot a glance at me over his shoulder. His eyes were asking, "And how do you expect me to do that?"

If Marley couldn't turn around, the airline was not letting him on the plane. I checked my watch. We had twelve minutes to make the flight.

"Come here, Marley!" I said more desperately. "Come on!" I snapped my fingers, rattled the metal gate, made kissy-kissy sounds. "Come on," I pleaded. "Turn around."

I was about to drop to my knees and beg when I heard a crash.

"Oops," Patrick said.

"The frogs are loose!" Jenny screamed, jumping into action.

"Froggy! Croaky! Come back!" the boys yelled in unison.

Jenny was on all fours now, racing around the termi-

Have bowl, will travel! Even as a puppy,
Marley loved sloshing water all over the house.

Marley gets comfortable in our backyard.

Marley on his first night at home,
crying to get out of his box.

No one loved the pool more than
Marley the torpedo dog.

Grogan's Majestic Marley of Churchill did have a
regal bearing—when he wasn't chasing his tail.

Marley exploring the garage on his first day home.

In hot southern Florida, Marley loved to
stretch out on the cool tile floor.

"Ah, nothing like a nice refreshing drink of saltwater."

Marley peers in from outside on the pool deck.

Sun, sand, surf—and his master, too. Life is good!

Marley relaxing on Dog Beach minutes before
throwing up in the water.

"Can you people please speak in dog?"

In his last year, Marley mostly slept.
This is our last photo of him, taken days
before we said our final good-byes.

nal. The frogs stayed one hop ahead of her. Passersby stopped and stared. From a distance you could not see the frogs at all, just the crazy lady with the diaper bag hanging from her neck. Looking at their faces, I could tell they fully expected her to start howling at any moment.

"Excuse me a second," I said as calmly as I could to the airline worker. Then I got down on my hands and knees, too.

Just as they were about to leap out the automatic doors, we captured Froggy and Croaky. As we turned back, I heard a mighty ruckus coming from the dog crate. The entire box shivered and lurched across the floor, and when I peered in I saw that Marley had somehow gotten himself turned around.

"See?" I said to the baggage supervisor. "He can turn around, no problem."

"Okay," she said with a frown. "But you're really pushing it."

Two workers lifted Marley and his crate onto a dolly and wheeled him away. The rest of us raced for our flight, arriving at the gate just as the flight attendants were closing the hatch.

"Wait! We're here!" I shouted, pushing Colleen

ahead of me. The boys and Jenny trailed by fifty feet.

As we settled into our seats, I breathed a sigh of relief. We had gotten Marley squared away. We had recaptured the frogs. We had made the flight. Next stop, Allentown, Pennsylvania. I could relax now.

Through the window I watched as a tram pulled up with the dog crate sitting on it. "Look," I said to the kids. "There's Marley." They waved out the window and called, "Hi, Waddy."

As the engines revved, I pulled out a magazine. That's when I noticed Jenny freeze in the row in front of me. Then I heard it, too. From below our feet, deep in the bowels of the plane, came a muffled sound. Starting low and mournful it rose as it went. *Oh, dear!* I thought. *He's down there howling.*

Just so you know, Labrador retrievers do not howl. Beagles howl. Wolves howl. Labs do not howl, at least not well. Marley had attempted to howl twice before, both times in answer to a passing police siren, tossing back his head, forming his mouth into an O shape, and letting loose the most pathetic sound I have ever heard, more like he was gargling than answering the call of the wild. But now, no question about it, he was howling.

The passengers began to look up from their newspapers and novels. A flight attendant handing out pillows paused and cocked her head quizzically.

"Listen. Do you hear that?" a woman across the aisle asked her husband. "I think it's a dog." Jenny stared straight ahead. I stared into my magazine. If anyone asked, we were denying ownership.

"Waddy's sad," Patrick said.

I just pulled my magazine higher over my face. The jet engines whined and the plane taxied down the runway, drowning out Marley. I pictured him down below in the dark hold, alone, scared, confused, not even able to stand up fully. I imagined the roaring engines. To Marley, they probably sounded like another thunderous assault by random lightning bolts determined to take him out. The poor guy. I knew I would be spending the whole flight worrying about him.

The airplane was barely off the ground when I heard another little crash.

"Oops," Conor said.

I looked down and then stared straight into my magazine. After several seconds, I glanced around. When I was pretty sure no one was staring, I leaned forward and whispered into Jenny's ear, "Don't look now, but the crickets are loose."

17

In the Land of Pencils

In Pennsylvania we moved into a rambling house with a huge yard. Our property had woods and a meadow where we could pick wild raspberries. Marley and the kids loved getting muddy in the small creek.

There was only one thing missing. Minutes after we pulled into the driveway of our new house, Conor looked up and declared, "I thought there were going to be pencils in Pencilvania." Big tears rolled from his eyes.

For our boys, now ages seven and five, this was a near deal breaker. Given the name of the state we were adopting, both of them arrived fully expecting to see bright yellow writing implements hanging like berries from every tree and shrub, there for the plucking. They were crushed to learn otherwise.

Marley, on the other hand, had no problem with our home. He fit right into the new country lifestyle. He raced across the lawn and crashed through the brambles.

The neighborhood rabbits considered my garden their own personal salad bar. Marley made it his mission to catch one of the diners. He would spot a rabbit munching the lettuce and barrel off down the hill in hot pursuit. His ears flapped behind him, his paws pounded the ground, and his bark filled the air. He was about as sneaky as a marching band. He never got closer than a dozen feet before his intended prey scampered off into the woods to safety. Five minutes later he'd do it all over again. Fortunately, he was no better at sneaking up on the skunks.

Autumn came and with it a whole new mischievous game: Attack the Leaf Pile. Trees did not shed their leaves in the fall in Florida. In Pennsylvania, Marley was positively convinced the falling leaves were a gift meant just for him.

As I raked the orange and yellow leaves into giant heaps, Marley would sit and watch patiently, waiting until just the right moment to attack. After I had gathered a towering pile, he would slink forward, crouched low. Every few steps, he would stop, front paw raised, to sniff the air like a lion stalking an unsuspecting gazelle. Then, just as I raked the last leaf, he would lunge. Charging across the lawn in a series of bounding leaps, he would fly for the last several feet and land in a giant belly flop in the middle of the pile. He growled and rolled and flailed and scratched and snapped and fiercely chased his tail, not stopping until my neat leaf pile was scattered across the lawn again. With the shredded remains of leaves clinging to his fur, he would sit up and give me a self-satisfied look, proud that he'd been such a big help.

Our first Christmas in Pennsylvania was supposed to be white. To convince Patrick and Conor to leave their home and friends in Florida, Jenny and I had promised them snow. As the holidays neared, the boys and Colleen sat in the window together for hours. "Come on, snow!" they chanted. They had never seen it.

Christmas morning they opened their gifts—a brand-new toboggan and enough snow gear to outfit an excursion to Antarctica. I built a cheery fire in the fireplace and told the children to be patient. The snow would come when the snow would come.

New Year's arrived, and still it did not come. Even Marley seemed antsy, pacing and gazing out the windows, whimpering softly. The kids returned to school after the holiday, and still nothing. They gazed sullenly at me at the breakfast table. I was the father who had betrayed them.

"Maybe little boys and girls in some other place need the snow more than we do," I suggested.

"Yeah, right, Dad," Patrick said.

A couple of weeks later, Patrick came running into our bedroom at dawn and yanked open the blinds. "Look! Look!" he squealed. "It's here!"

Jenny and I sat up in bed. A white blanket covered the hillsides and cornfields and pine trees and rooftops. "Of course it's here," I answered. "What did I tell you?"

The snow was nearly a foot deep and still coming down. Soon Conor and Colleen came chugging down the hall, thumbs in mouths, blankies trailing behind them. Sensing the excitement, Marley was up and stretching, banging his tail into everything.

"I guess going back to sleep isn't an option," I told Jenny.

"No, it's not," she said.

"Okay, snow bunnies, let's suit up!" I shouted.

For the next half hour we wrestled with zippers and buckles and hats and gloves. By the time we were done, the kids looked like mummies.

I opened the front door, and before anyone else could step out, Marley blasted past us, knocking Colleen down. The instant his paws hit the foreign white stuff, he had second thoughts. "Ah, wet! Ah, cold!" He attempted an abrupt about-face. But stopping *and* turning at the same time on slippery snow was *not* a good idea.

Marley went into a full skid, his rear end spinning out in front of him. He dropped down on his side briefly before bouncing upright again, just in time to somersault down the front porch steps and dive headfirst into a snowdrift. When he popped back up a second later, he looked like a giant powdered doughnut. Except for a black nose and two brown eyes, he was completely dusted in white. The Abominable Snowdog.

Marley did not know what to make of this strange substance. He jammed his nose deep into it and let out a violent sneeze. He snapped at it and rubbed his face in it. Then he took off at full throttle, racing around the yard in a series of giant, loping leaps. Every several feet he tumbled into a somersault or took a nosedive. Snow was almost as much fun as raiding the neighbors' trash.

Marley's tracks in the snow told us a lot about his warped mind. His path was filled with abrupt twists and turns and about-faces, with erratic loops and figure eights, corkscrews, and triple lutzes. Soon the kids were following his lead, spinning and rolling and frolicking, snow packing into every crease and crevice of their outerwear.

Jenny came out with buttered toast and mugs of hot cocoa. "School's closed," she announced. The first snow day of our children's lives was now perfect.

I scraped the snow away from the stone circle I had built that fall for backyard campfires and soon had a crackling blaze going.

The kids glided screaming down the hill in the toboggan, past the campfire and to the edge of the woods. Marley chased behind.

When the three of them took a break, to get warm

by the fire, I decided to try a run on the toboggan.

"Care to join me?" I asked Jenny.

"Sorry, you're on your own," she said.

I positioned the toboggan at the top of the hill and lay back on it, propped up on my elbows with my feet tucked inside its nose. I began rocking to get moving. Marley rarely got a chance to look down at me. Lying on my back was like delivering an invitation to him. He crept up close to me and sniffed my face.

"What do you want?" I asked. That was all the welcome he needed. He climbed aboard, straddling me and dropping onto my chest. "Get off me, you big lug!" I screamed. But it was too late. We were already creeping forward, gathering speed as we began our descent.

"Bon voyage!" Jenny yelled behind us.

Off we went, snow flying, Marley plastered on top of me, licking me all over the face as we headed down the slope. We weighed more than the kids, so we went a lot faster—and a lot farther.

"Hold on, Marley!" I screamed. "We're going into the woods!"

We shot past a large walnut tree, then between two wild cherry trees. We crashed through the underbrush, brambles tearing at us. Suddenly I remembered the creek up ahead, still unfrozen. There was a steep bank that led down to it. And we were going over. I tried to kick my feet out to use as brakes, but they were stuck.

I wrapped my arms around Marley, squeezed my eyes shut, and yelled, "Whoaaaaaa!"

Our toboggan shot over the bank and dropped out from under us. In a Scooby-Doo moment, we hovered in midair for an endless second before falling. But instead of Scooby-Doo, I had a madly salivating Labrador retriever welded to me. We clung to each other as we crash-landed into a snowbank with a soft *poof* and, hanging half off the toboggan, slid to the water's edge.

Marley was up and prancing around me, eager to do it all over again. But not me.

"I'm getting too old for this stuff," I said.

In the months ahead it would become clear that Marley was, too.

Our dog had turned nine that first winter in Pennsylvania, and he was slowing down. He still had his bursts of adrenalin-pumped energy, but the bursts were briefer now and farther apart. He was happy to snooze most of the day, and on walks he got tired before I did.

That had never happened before.

One late-winter day, I walked him down our hill and up the next one, even steeper than ours. We'd done it many times before, and Marley had always led the charge to the top without really trying. This time, though, he was falling behind.

"Come on, boy. You can do it!" I coaxed him along.

Marley just did not have the oomph needed to make it to the top. It was like watching a toy slowly wind down as its battery went dead. He stopped and sat down.

"You're not going soft on me, are you?" I asked. I leaned over to stroke his face with my gloved hands. He looked up at me, his eyes bright, his nose wet. He was tuckered, but he couldn't have been happier. For Marley, life got no better than this, sitting along the side of a country road on a crisp day with your master.

"If you think I'm carrying you, forget it," I said.

In the bright sunshine, I could see just how much gray had crept into his big yellow face. His whole muzzle and a good part of his brow had turned from buff to white. Without our quite realizing it, our eternal puppy had become an old dog.

That's not to say Marley behaved any better. He was

still up to all his old tricks. He just took his time doing them. He still stole food off the children's plates. He still flipped open the lid to the kitchen trash can with his nose and rummaged inside. He still strained at his leash. Still swallowed all kinds of household objects. Still drank out of the bathtub and trailed water from his mouth. And when the skies darkened and thunder rumbled, he still panicked. If he was alone when storm clouds rolled in, he still turned destructive. One day we arrived home to find Marley all upset—and Conor's mattress ripped open down to the coils.

Over the years, we had come to accept the damage, which had become much less frequent now that we were away from Florida's daily storms. In a dog's life, some plaster would fall, some cushions would get ripped open, some rugs would shred. They were costs we came to balance against the joy and laughter and protection and companionship he gave us. We could have bought a yacht with what we spent on our dog and all the things he destroyed. We'd take Marley any day. Yachts don't wait by the door all day for your return. And they don't live for the moment they can climb into your lap or ride down the hill with you on a toboggan, licking your face.

18

Poultry on Parade

That spring we decided to try our hand at animal husbandry. We owned two acres in the country now. It only seemed right to share it with a farm animal or two. We just had to figure out which kind.

"A cow would be fun," Jenny suggested.

"A cow?" I asked. "Are you crazy? We don't even have a barn. How can we have a cow? Where would we keep it, in the garage next to the minivan?"

"How about sheep? Sheep are cute," she said.

I shot her my best you're-not-being-practical look.
"A goat?" she asked. "Goats are adorable."
In the end we decided on poultry.

Yes, chickens it was. Jenny had become friendly with a mom from school who lived on a farm. She said she'd be happy to give us some chicks from the next clutch of eggs to hatch.

Our neighbor, Digger, had a large coop of his own in which he kept a flock of chickens for both eggs and meat. I told him about our plans. He agreed a few hens around the place made sense.

"Just one word of warning," he said, folding his meaty arms across his chest. "Whatever you do, don't let the kids name them. Once you name 'em, they're no longer poultry. They're pets."

"Right," I said. Hens could live fifteen years or more, but they laid eggs only in their first couple years. When they stopped laying, they ended up in the stewing pot. That was just part of managing a flock.

Digger looked hard at me. "Once you name them, it's all over," he repeated.

"Absolutely," I agreed. "No names."

The next evening I pulled into the driveway from

work, and the three kids raced out of the house to greet me. Each cradled a newborn chick. Jenny was behind them with a fourth in her hands. Her friend Donna had brought over the baby birds that afternoon. They were barely a day old and peered up at me with cocked heads. "Are you my mama?" they seemed to ask.

Patrick was the first to break the news. "I named mine Feathers," he proclaimed.

"Mine is Tweety," said Conor.

"My wicka Wuffy," Colleen chimed in.

I shot Jenny a quizzical look.

"Fluffy," Jenny said. "She named her chicken Fluffy."

"Jenny," I protested. "What did Digger tell us? These are farm animals, not pets."

"Oh, get real, Farmer John," she said. "You know as well as I do that you could never hurt one of these. Just look at how cute they are."

"Jenny," I said, the frustration rising in my voice.

Jenny held up the fourth chick. "By the way," she said, "meet Shirley."

Feathers, Tweety, Fluffy, and Shirley lived in a box on the kitchen counter. A lightbulb dangled above them for warmth. They ate and they pooped and they ate some more. And they grew—fast.

Several weeks after we brought the birds home, something jolted me awake. It was before dawn. I sat up in bed and listened. From downstairs came a weak, sickly call. It was croaky and hoarse.

"Cock-a-doodle-do!" it sounded again. A few seconds ticked past.

Then came an equally sickly reply. "Rook-ru-rook-ru-roo!"

I shook Jenny. "When Donna brought the chicks over, you did ask her to check to make sure they were girls, right?" I said.

"You mean you can do that?" she asked. She rolled back over and fell sound asleep.

It turned out that three of our four "laying hens" were males. And males did not make eggs. Mostly, they made noise.

I thought the constant crowing of our roosters would drive Marley insane. In his younger years, the sweet chirp of a single tiny songbird in the yard would set him off on a wild barking jag as he raced from one window to the next, hopping up and down on his hind legs. Three crowing roosters a few steps from his food bowl, however, had no effect on him at all. He didn't even seem to know they were there. Each day the crowing grew louder and stronger. At five in the morning, the noise rose from the kitchen to echo through the house. "Cock-a-doodle-dooooo!" Marley slept right through the racket.

That's when it first occurred to me that maybe he wasn't just ignoring the crowing. Maybe he couldn't hear it.

I walked up behind him one afternoon as he snoozed in the kitchen. "Marley?" Nothing. I said it louder. "Marley!" Nothing. I clapped my hands and shouted, "MARLEY!" He lifted his head and looked blankly around, his ears up, trying to figure out what his radar had detected. I did it again, clapping loudly and shouting his name. This time he turned his head enough to catch a glimpse of me standing behind him.

Marley bounced up, tail wagging, happy to see me. "Oh, it's you!" the surprised expression on his face said. He bumped against my legs in greeting and gave me a sheepish look, as if to ask, "What's the idea sneaking up on me like that?"

My dog, it seemed, was going deaf.

It all made sense. In recent months, Marley had seemed to ignore me in a way he never had before. I would call for him, and he wouldn't even glance my way. I would take him outside before going to bed. He would sniff his way across the yard, oblivious to my whistles and calls to get him to turn back. And when he was asleep at my feet in the family room and someone rang the doorbell, he wouldn't even open an eye.

Not that he seemed to mind. Retirement suited Marley just fine. His hearing problems did not stop him from taking life easy. And now deafness finally gave him an excuse for disobeying. After all, how could he obey what he couldn't hear? He may have been thick skulled, but he was smart enough to figure out how to use his deafness to his advantage. Drop a piece of steak in his bowl, and he would come trotting in from the next room. He still had the ability to detect the dull, satisfying thud of meat on metal. But when I yelled for him to come, he'd stroll away from me—especially when he had somewhere else he'd rather go. He didn't even glance guiltily over his shoulder like he used to.

"I think the dog's fooling us," I told Jenny.

"His hearing problems do seem to come and go whenever it suits him," she agreed. But every time we tested him, sneaking up, clapping our hands, shouting his name, he would not respond. And every time we dropped food in his bowl, he would come running. He appeared to be deaf to all sounds except the one that was dearest to his heart or, more accurately, his stomach—the sound of dinner.

Marley went through life hungry. We gave him four big scoops of dog chow a day—enough food to keep an entire family of Chihuahuas going for a week. We also began giving him table scraps, even though every dog guide we had ever read told us not to. Table scraps programmed dogs to prefer human food to dog chow. (Given the choice between a half-eaten hamburger and dry kibble, who could blame them?) Table scraps were a recipe for chubby canines.

Not our dog. Marley had many problems, but obesity was not one of them. No matter how many calories he devoured, he always burned more. All that high-strung exuberance ate up lots of energy. He was like a high-kilowatt electric plant that instantly converted every ounce of available fuel into pure, raw power.

Marley was an amazing physical specimen, the kind of dog passersby stopped to admire. He was huge for a Labrador retriever, considerably bigger than the average male of his breed, which weighs between sixty-five and eighty pounds. Marley was ninety-seven pounds of pure muscle. We were not worried about him getting fat.

Each evening after the family finished dinner, I filled Marley's bowl with chow, then freely tossed in any tasty leftovers or scraps I could find. With three young children at the table, we had plenty of half-eaten food. Bread crusts, steak trimmings, pan drippings, chicken skin, gravy, rice, carrots, pureed prunes, sandwiches, three-day-old pasta. Into the bowl they went. We kept dairy products, sweets, potatoes, and chocolate from him because those were unhealthy for dogs. But that was just about all he couldn't have.

When Marley wasn't acting as our household garbage disposal, he was on duty as the family's emergency spill response team. No mess was too big a job for our dog. One of the kids would flip a full bowl of spaghetti and meatballs on the floor, and we'd simply whistle and stand back as Old Wet Vac sucked up every last noodle. Then he would lick the floor until it gleamed. Escaped peas, dropped celery, runaway rigatoni, spilled applesauce, it didn't matter what it was. If it hit the floor, it was history. To the amazement of our friends, he even wolfed down salad greens.

Not that food had to make it to the ground before it ended up in Marley's stomach. He was a skilled and unremorseful thief. Unsuspecting children were his favorite target—after he checked to make sure neither Jenny nor I was watching.

Birthday parties were bonanzas for him. He would make his way through the crowd of five-year-olds, shamelessly snatching hot dogs right out of their hands. During one party, we estimated he ended up getting two-thirds of the birthday cake, nabbing piece after piece off the paper plates the children held on their laps.

It didn't matter how much food he devoured, either through legitimate means or theft. He always wanted more.

One day I arrived home from work to find the house empty. Jenny and the kids were out somewhere.

"Marley," I called. No response.

I walked upstairs, where he sometimes snoozed, but he was nowhere in sight. After I changed my clothes, I returned downstairs and found him in the kitchen up to no good. With his back to me, he was standing on his hind legs. His front paws and chest rested on the kitchen table as he gobbled down the remains of a grilled cheese sandwich. I decided to see how close I could get before he realized he had company. I tiptoed up behind him until I was close enough to touch him.

As he chewed the crusts, he kept glancing at the door that led into the garage. He knew that was where Jenny and the kids would enter when they returned. The instant the door opened, he would be on the floor under the table, pretending to be asleep. He hadn't figured out that Dad would be arriving home, too, and just might sneak in through the front door.

"Oh, Marley?" I asked in a normal voice. "What do you think you're doing?" He just kept gulping down the sandwich, clueless to my presence. His tail was wagging lazily, a sign he thought he was alone and getting away with a major food heist. He clearly was pleased with himself.

I cleared my throat loudly, and he still did not hear me. I made kissy noises with my mouth. Nothing. He polished off one sandwich, nosed the plate out of the way, and stretched forward to reach the crusts left on a second plate.

"You are such a bad dog," I said as he chewed away.

I snapped my fingers twice and he froze midbite, staring at the back door. "What was that? Did I hear a car door slam?" After a moment, he decided that whatever he had heard was nothing and went back to his stolen snack.

That's when I reached out and tapped him once on the butt. I might as well have lit off a stick of dynamite. The old dog nearly jumped out of his fur coat. He rocketed backward off the table. As soon as he saw me, he dropped onto the floor, rolling over to expose his belly to me in surrender.

"Busted!" I told him. "You are so busted." But I didn't have it in me to scold him. He was old. He was deaf. He would never reform. I wasn't going to change him. Sneaking up on him had been great fun, and I laughed out loud when he jumped. Now as he lay at my feet begging for forgiveness, I just found it a little sad. I guess secretly I had hoped he had been faking all along.

I built a chicken coop so our newest family members could safely live outside. Donna kindly took back two of our three roosters and exchanged them for hens from her flock. We now had three girls and one loudmouth guy bird.

We let the chickens out each morning to roam the yard, and Marley made a few gallant runs at them. He charged ahead, barking as he ran about a dozen paces. Then he'd lose steam and give up. Something deep inside him said, "You're a retriever; they are birds. Don't you think it might be a good idea to chase them?" But his heart just wasn't in it.

Soon the birds learned that the lumbering yellow beast was no threat—more a minor annoyance than anything else. Marley learned to share the yard with these new, feathered interlopers. One day I looked up from weeding in the garden to see Marley and the four chickens making their way down the row toward me as if in formation. The birds pecked and Marley sniffed as they went. It was like old friends out for a Sunday stroll.

"What kind of self-respecting hunting dog are you?" I scolded him. Marley lifted his leg and peed on a tomato plant before hurrying to rejoin his new pals.

19

The Potty Room

Marley aged about seven years for every one of ours. In human years, he was close to ninety. His once sparkling white teeth had gradually worn down to brown nubs. Three of his four front fangs were missing, broken off one by one during crazed panic attacks as he tried to chew his way to China. His breath was always a bit on the fishy side. Now it had taken on the scent of rotting garbage. It didn't help that he had taken to gobbling up chicken manure like it was caviar.

Marley's digestion was not what it once had been, and he became as gassy as a methane plant. There were days I swore that if I lit a match the whole house would go up. Marley was able to clear an entire room with one silent, deadly fart. The more visitors we had, the more he let them rip.

"Marley! Not again!" the children would scream in unison and lead the retreat out of the room.

Sometimes he drove even himself away. He would be sleeping peacefully when the smell would reach his nostrils. His eyes would pop open and he'd scrunch up his brow as if asking, "Who dealt *that*?" Then he would stand up and casually move into the next room.

When Marley wasn't farting, he was outside pooping. Or at least thinking about it. Each time I let him out, he took longer and longer to decide on just the perfect spot. Back and forth he would walk. Round and round he went, sniffing, pausing, scratching, circling, and moving on. The entire time he wore a ridiculous grin on his face. I stood outside, sometimes in the rain, sometimes in the snow, sometimes in the dark of night, often barefoot, occasionally just in my underwear. I didn't dare leave him unsupervised or he might head up the hill to visit the dogs on the next street.

Sneaking away became a sport for him. If he had the chance and thought he could get away with it, he would bolt for the property line. Well, not exactly bolt. He would sniff and shuffle his way from one bush to the next until he was out of sight.

Late one night, I let him out the front door for his final walk of the night. Freezing rain was falling, forming an icy slush on the ground. I turned around to grab a raincoat out of the front closet. When I walked out on the sidewalk less than a minute later, he was nowhere to be found. I went into the yard, whistling and clapping, knowing he couldn't hear me, but I was pretty sure all the neighbors could. For twenty minutes, I prowled through our neighbors' yards in the rain—dressed in boots, raincoat, and boxer shorts. I prayed no porch lights would come on. The more I hunted, the angrier I got. But as the minutes passed, my anger turned to worry.

I returned home and woke up Jenny. "Marley's disappeared," I said. "I can't find him anywhere. He's out there in the freezing rain."

Jenny was on her feet instantly, pulling on jeans, slipping into a sweater and boots. Together we broadened the search. I could hear her way up the side of the hill, whistling and clucking for him as I crashed through the woods in the dark.

Eventually our paths met up. "Anything?" I asked.

"Nothing," Jenny said. We were soaked from the rain, and my bare legs were stinging from the cold.

"Come on," I said. "Let's go home and get warm and I'll come back out with the car." We returned down the hill and up the driveway.

That's when we saw him, standing beneath the over-hang out of the rain and overjoyed to have us back. I could have killed him. Instead I brought him inside and toweled him off. The unmistakable smell of wet dog filled the kitchen. Exhausted from his late-night jaunt, Marley conked out and did not budge till nearly noon the next day.

Marley's eyesight had grown fuzzy. Bunnies scampered just a dozen feet away, and he didn't notice. He shed huge amounts of fur. Dog hair made its way into every crevice of our home, every piece of our clothing, and more than a few of our meals. He would shake and a cloud of loose fur would rise around him, drifting down onto every surface. One night as I watched television, I dangled my leg off the couch and absently stroked his hip with my bare foot. At the commercial break, I looked down to see a sphere of fur the size of a grape-fruit near where I had been rubbing. His hairballs rolled across the wood floors like tumbleweeds on a wind-blown plain.

Most worrisome of all were his hips. Arthritis had snuck into his joints, making them weak and achy. When he was young, I used to ride on his back like a cowboy on a horse. He had lifted the entire dining-room table on his shoulders and bounced it around the room. Now he could barely pull himself up. He groaned in pain when he lay down, and groaned again when he struggled to his feet. I did not realize just how weak his hips had become until one day when I gave his rump a light pat. His hindquarters collapsed beneath him as though he had just received a cross-body block. Down he went. It was painful to watch.

Climbing the stairs to the second floor was tough, too. But Marley would not think of sleeping alone on the main floor, even after we put a dog bed at the foot of the stairs for him. He loved people, loved being underfoot, loved resting his chin on the mattress and panting in our faces as we slept. He loved jamming his head through the shower curtain for a drink as we bathed, and he wasn't about to stop now. Each night when Jenny and I went to bed, he would fret at the foot of the stairs, whining, yipping, and pacing.

"Come on, boy. You can do it," I called from the top of the stairs. After several minutes of this, he would disappear around the corner in order to get a running start and then come charging up. Sometimes he made it. Sometimes he got only halfway and had to return to the bottom and try again. On his most pitiful attempts, he would lose his footing entirely and slide backward down the steps on his belly. He was too big for me to carry, so I followed him up the stairs, lifting his rear end up each step as he hopped forward on his front paws.

Did all of this trouble stop Marley? Not a chance. That would be giving him far too much credit for common sense. No matter how much trouble he had getting up the stairs, if I returned downstairs, he would be right on my heels, clomping heavily down behind me. I might only have to grab a book or turn off the lights. So seconds later he would have to repeat the torturous climb again. Jenny and I started sneaking around behind his back once he was upstairs for the night. We didn't want him to follow us back down. It hardly ever worked. He always seemed to know when we had snuck off.

I would be reading in bed and he would be asleep on the floor beside me, snoring heavily. Slowly, I would pull back the covers, slide out of bed, and tiptoe past him out of the room, turning back to make sure I had not disturbed him. I would be downstairs for only a few seconds when I would hear his heavy steps on the stairs, coming in search of me. He might be deaf and half blind, but Marley's radar worked just fine.

This went on all day long, too. I would be reading the newspaper at the kitchen table with Marley curled up at my feet. I'd get up for a refill from the coffeepot across the room. I was within sight and would be coming right back, but Marley didn't know it. Very slowly he would get on his feet and trudge over to be with me. Just as he got comfortable at my feet by the coffeepot, it would be time for me to return to the table. So he would again drag himself up and settle in next to me. A few minutes later, I would walk into the family room to turn on the stereo. He would struggle up again. He'd follow me in, then circle around and collapse with a moan beside me—just as I was ready to walk away.

Marley had good days and bad days. He had good minutes and bad minutes, too. They happened so close together, sometimes it was hard to believe it was the same dog.

One evening in the spring of 2002, I took Marley out for a short walk around the yard. The night was cool and windy. I started to run, and Marley galloped along beside me just like in the old days.

"See, Marl, you still have some of the puppy in you," I told him. We trotted together back to the front door, his tongue out as he panted happily, his eyes alert.

Marley tried to leap up the two porch steps—but his rear hips collapsed on him as he pushed off. He was stuck. With his front paws on the stoop, his belly rested on the steps and his butt collapsed flat on the sidewalk. There he sat, looking up at me like he didn't know what had caused such an embarrassing display. I whistled and slapped my hands on my thighs. Using all his might, he flailed his front legs, trying to get up. But it was no use. He could not lift his rear off the ground.

"Come on, Marley!" I called, but he was immobilized. Finally I grabbed him under the front shoulders and turned him sideways so he could get all four legs on the ground. After a few tries, he was able to stand up. He backed up, looked at the stairs for a few seconds, and loped up and into the house. From that day on, his confidence as a champion stair climber was shot. He never attempted those two small steps again without first stopping and fretting.

No doubt about it, getting old was no fun. No fun at all.

By November 2002, I had found another new job, writing for the *Philadelphia Inquirer*. I had been in the new job only a few months when the first big snowstorm of 2003 hit.

The flakes began to fall on a Sunday night, and by the time they stopped the next day, a blanket two feet deep covered the ground. The children were off school for three days. With a snowblower borrowed from my neighbor, I cleared the driveway and opened a narrow canyon to the front door. I knew Marley could never climb the steep walls to get out into the yard, let alone make his way through the deep drifts once he was off the path. So I cleared a small space off the front walkway where he could do his business. The kids called it his potty room.

I called him outside to try it out. He just stood in the clearing and sniffed the snow suspiciously. He had very particular ideas about where he could and could not go. This clearly was not what he had in mind. He was willing to lift his leg and pee, but that's where he drew the line. He looked up at me as if to say, "Poop right here? Smack in front of the picture window? You can't be serious." He turned away and went back inside.

That night after dinner I brought him out again. This time Marley couldn't wait. He had to go. He nervously paced up and down the cleared walkway, into the potty room and out onto the driveway. Sniffing the snow and pawing at the frozen ground was his way of saying, "No, this just won't do."

Before I could stop him, he somehow scrambled up and over the snow wall the snowblower had cut. He began making his way across the yard toward a stand of white pines fifty feet away. I could not believe it. My arthritic old dog was off on an alpine trek. Every couple steps his back hips collapsed on him and he sank down into the snow. There he rested on his belly for a few seconds before struggling back to his feet and pushing on. Slowly, painfully, he made his way through the deep snow, using his still-strong front shoulders to pull his body forward. I stood in the driveway, wondering how I was going to rescue him when he finally got stuck and could go no farther. But he trudged on and finally made it to the closest pine tree. Suddenly I saw what he was up to. The dog had a plan.

Beneath the dense branches of the pine, the snow was just a few inches deep. The tree acted like an umbrella. Marley was free to move about and squat comfortably to relieve himself. I had to admit, it was pretty brilliant. He circled and sniffed and scratched in his customary way, trying to locate a worthy shrine for his daily offering. Then, to my amazement, he abandoned the cozy shelter and lunged back into the deep snow, on his way to the next pine tree. The first spot looked perfect to me, but clearly it wasn't up to his standards.

The second tree was also tough for Marley to get to. But after a lot of circling, he again decided the area beneath its branches wasn't quite right. So he set off to the third tree, and then the fourth and the fifth, each time getting farther from the driveway. I tried calling him back, though I knew he could not hear me.

"Marley, you're going to get stuck, you dumbo," I yelled. He just plowed ahead. The dog was on a quest. Finally he reached the last tree on our property, a big spruce with a dense canopy of branches. It was near where the kids waited for the school bus. Here he found the frozen piece of ground he had been looking for, private and barely dusted with snow. He circled a few times and creakily squatted down on his old, shot, arthritis-riddled haunches. There he finally found relief. Eureka!

With mission accomplished, he set off on the long journey home.

"Keep coming, boy!" I called. "You can make it!" As he struggled through the snow, I waved my arms and clapped my hands to encourage him. But I could see him tiring, and he still had a long way to go. "Don't stop now," I yelled.

A dozen yards from the driveway, that's just what he did. He was done. He stopped and lay down in the snow, exhausted. Marley did not exactly look distressed, but he did not look at ease, either. He shot me a worried look that said, "Now what do we do, boss?"

I had no idea. I could wade through the snow to him, but then what? He was too heavy for me to pick up and carry. For several minutes, I stood there, calling and cajoling, but Marley would not budge.

"Hang on," I said. "Let me get my boots on and I'll come get you." I grabbed the toboggan, figuring I could wrestle him onto it and pull him back to the house.

But as soon as he saw me approaching with the toboggan, Marley suddenly jumped up, reenergized. He must have remembered our ride into the woods and over the creek bank. He was probably hoping to do it again. He lurched forward toward me like a dinosaur in a tar pit. I waded out into the snow, stomping down a path for him as I went, and he inched ahead. Finally we scrambled over the snowbank and onto the driveway together. He shook off the snow and banged his tail against my knees, prancing about, all frisky and cocky, flush with the bravado of an adventurer just back from a jaunt through uncharted wilderness. To think I had doubted he could do it.

The next morning I shoveled a narrow path out to the far spruce tree on the corner of the property for him. Marley adopted the space as his own personal toilet for the rest of the winter. The crisis had been averted, but bigger questions loomed. How much longer could he continue on like this? And at what point would the aches of old age outstrip the happiness he found in each sleepy, lazy day?

20

Beating the Odds

When school let out for the summer, Jenny packed the kids into the minivan and headed to Boston for a week to visit her sister. I stayed behind to work. With Jenny and the kids away, I knew I would be putting in long days. We decided to board Marley at the local kennel we used every summer when we went on vacation.

"Waddy go doggie camp!" Colleen screeched.

Marley perked up as though he thought Colleen had a pretty good idea. We joked about the activities the kennel staff would have for him—hole digging from nine to ten, pillow shredding from 10:15 to eleven, garbage raiding from 11:05 to noon. The truth was, Marley never seemed to relax when he was at the kennel. I always worried a little about him.

I dropped him off on a Sunday evening and left my cell-phone number with the front desk. On Tuesday morning of that week, I was seeing the sights in downtown Philadelphia when my cell phone rang.

"Hello?" I answered.

"Could you please hold for Dr. Hopkinson?" the woman from the kennel asked. A few seconds later the vet came on the phone.

"We have an emergency with Marley," she said.

My heart rose in my chest. "An emergency?"

Dr. Hopkinson said Marley's stomach had bloated with food, water, and air. It had flipped over on itself, twisting and trapping its contents. With nowhere for the gas and other contents to escape, his stomach had swelled painfully, in a life-threatening condition.

"It almost always requires surgery to correct," she said. She added that a dog could die if the problem wasn't fixed.

The vet said she had inserted a tube down Marley's

throat and released much of the gas that had built up in his stomach. That relieved the swelling. By manipulating the tube, she thought she had worked the twist out of his stomach, or as she put it, "unflipped it." Now he was sedated and resting comfortably.

"That's a good thing, right?" I asked cautiously.

"But only temporary," the doctor said. "We got him through the immediate crisis, but once their stomachs twist like that, they almost always will twist again."

"Like how almost always?" I asked.

"I would say he has a one percent chance that it won't flip again," she said.

"One percent? That's it?"

"I'm sorry," she said. "It's very grave."

If his stomach did flip again, we had two choices. The first was to operate on him.

"The operation will cost about two thousand dollars," she said. I gulped. "And I have to tell you, it's very invasive. It will be tough going for a dog his age." The recovery would be long and difficult—assuming he made it through the operation at all. Sometimes older dogs like him did not survive the trauma of the surgery, she explained.

"If he were four or five years old, I would be saying

by all means let's operate," the vet said. "But at his age, you have to ask yourself if you really want to put him through that."

"Not if we can help it," I said. "What's the second option?"

"The second option," she said, hesitating only slightly, "would be putting him to sleep."

"Oh," I said.

I was having trouble processing it all. Five minutes ago, I was walking to the Liberty Bell assuming Marley was resting in his kennel run. Now I was being asked to decide whether he would live or die. I had never even heard of the condition she described. Later I learned that bloat is fairly common in some breeds of dogs, especially those with deep barrel chests. Dogs who scarfed down their entire meal in a few quick gulps also seemed to be at higher risk. Marley definitely fit the description.

Dr. Hopkinson agreed that Marley's excitement around the other dogs in the kennel could have brought on the attack. He had gulped down his food as usual, and was panting and salivating heavily, worked up by all the other dogs around him. All that might have caused the problem.

"Can't we just wait and see how he does?" I asked. "Maybe it won't twist again."

"That's what we're doing right now—waiting and watching," she said. "If his stomach flips again, I'll need you to make a quick decision. We can't let him suffer."

"I need to speak with my wife," I told her. "I'll call you back."

I called Jenny on her cell phone and explained the situation. There was silence on the other end.

"Hello? Are you still there?" I asked.

"I'm here," Jenny said, then went quiet again. By the end of the conversation, we decided there was really no decision at all. The vet was right. Marley was thirteen years old and fading on all fronts. It would be cruel to put him through traumatic surgery. No matter what, he was close to the end of his life. If this was Marley's time, then it was his time. It was our responsibility to make sure he didn't suffer. We knew it was the right thing—even though neither of us was ready to lose him.

I called the veterinarian back and told her our decision. "His teeth are rotted away, he's stone deaf, and his hips have gotten so bad he can barely get up the porch stoop anymore," I explained. "He's having trouble squatting to have a bowel movement."

Dr. Hopkinson made it easy on me. "I think it's time," she said.

"I guess so," I answered, but I did not want her to put him down without calling me first. I wanted to be there with him if possible. "And," I reminded her, "I'm still holding out for that one-percent miracle."

"Let's talk in an hour," she said.

An hour later, Dr. Hopkinson sounded slightly more optimistic. Marley was still holding his own. Nourishment dripped into his body through a tube in his front leg. She raised his odds to five percent. "I don't want you to get your hopes up," she said. "He's a very sick dog."

The next morning, the doctor sounded brighter still. "He had a good night," she said. When I called back at noon, she had removed the tube from his leg and started him on a soupy mix of rice and meat. "He's famished," she reported.

By the next call, Marley was up on his feet. "Good news," the vet said. "One of our techs just took him outside and he pooped and peed." I cheered into the phone as though he had just finished first in the dog show. "He must be feeling better," she added. "He just gave me a big sloppy kiss on the lips." Yep, that was our Marley.

"Yesterday I didn't think it was possible," the doc said. "But I think you'll be able to take him home tomorrow."

The following evening after work, that's just what I did. He looked terrible—weak and skeletal. His eyes were milky and crusted with mucus.

"The whole staff loves Marley," the doctor told me. "Everyone was rooting for him."

I walked him out to the car. My miracle dog had beaten the odds.

"Let's get you home where you belong," I said. He just stood there looking woefully into the backseat. To him, it was as impossible to climb as Mount Olympus. He didn't even try to hop in. I called to one of the kennel workers, who helped me carefully lift him into the car.

I drove him home with a box of medicines and strict instructions. Marley would never again gulp a huge meal in one sitting, nor slurp unlimited amounts of water. His days of playing submarine with his snout in the water bowl were over. From now on, he would receive four small meals a day. He'd get small amounts of water—a half cup or so in his bowl at a time. The goal was to keep his stomach calm so it wouldn't twist again. And he wouldn't be staying in a large kennel surrounded by barking dogs ever again. Dr. Hopkinson and I were convinced it was the big reason for his close call with death.

That night, after I got him home and inside, I spread a sleeping bag on the floor in the family room beside him. He was still too weak to climb the stairs to the bedroom. I didn't have the heart to leave him alone and helpless.

"We're having a sleepover, Marley!" I proclaimed, and lay down beside him. I stroked him head to tail until huge clouds of fur rolled off his back. I wiped the mucus from the corners of his eyes and scratched his ears until he moaned with pleasure.

Jenny and the kids would be home in the morning. She would pamper him with frequent minimeals of boiled hamburger and rice. The children would throw their arms around him, unaware of how close they had come to never seeing him again.

Tomorrow the house would be loud and boisterous and full of life again. For tonight, it was just the two of us, Marley and me. Lying there with him, his smelly breath in my face, I could not help thinking of our first night together all those years ago when I had brought him home from the breeder, a tiny puppy whimpering for his mother. I remembered how I had dragged his box into the bedroom and the way we had fallen asleep together, my arm dangling over the side of the bed to comfort him. Thirteen years later, here we were, still inseparable. I thought about his puppyhood and adolescence, about the shredded couches and eaten mattresses, about the wild walks and cheek-to-jowl dances with the stereo blaring. I thought about the swallowed objects and sweet moments of canine-human friendship. Mostly I thought about what a good and loyal companion he had been all these years. What a trip it had been.

"You really scared me, old man," I whispered. He stretched out beside me and slid his snout beneath my arm to encourage me to keep petting him. "It's good to have you home."

Marley and I fell asleep together there, side by side on the floor. His rump was half on my sleeping bag. My arm was draped across his back. He woke me once in the night, his shoulders flinching, his paws twitching, little baby barks coming from deep in his throat. He was dreaming. Dreaming, I imagined, that he was young and strong again. And running like there was no tomorrow.

21

Borrowed Time

Over the next several weeks, Marley bounced back from the edge of death. The mischievous sparkle returned to his eyes, the cool wetness to his nose, and a little meat to his bones. He was content to snooze his days away in front of the glass door in the family room where the sun flooded in and baked his fur.

On his new diet, he was perpetually hungry. He begged and stole food more shamelessly than ever. One evening I caught him alone in the kitchen, up on his hind legs with his front paws on the kitchen counter, stealing Rice Krispies Treats from a platter. How he got up there, I'll never know. He could barely walk on his frail hips, but that didn't stop him. When the will called, Marley's body answered. I wanted to hug him, I was so happy at the surprise display of strength.

In many ways, he was still the same happy-go-lucky dog. Each morning after his breakfast, he trotted into the family room to use the couch as a giant napkin. He walked along its length, rubbing his snout and mouth against the fabric as he went and flipping up the cushions in the process. Then he would turn around and come back in the opposite direction so he could wipe the other side. From there he would drop to the floor and roll onto his back, wiggling from side to side to give himself a back rub. He liked to sit and lick the carpeting, as if it had been coated with the most delectable gravy he had ever tasted.

Marley's daily routine included barking at the mailman, visiting the chickens, staring at the birdfeeder, and checking the bathtub faucets for any drips of water he could lap up. Several times a day, he flipped up the lid on the kitchen trash can to see what goodies he could scavenge. On a daily basis, he launched into Labrador evader mode, banging around the house, tail thumping the walls and furniture. And on a daily basis I continued to pry open his jaws and pull out all sorts of odds and ends from the roof of his mouth—potato skins and muffin wrappers, discarded Kleenex and dental floss. Even in old age, some things didn't change.

In September 2003, I traveled out of town to work on a column I was writing. After I finished, I called home from the hotel.

"I just want you to know that Marley really misses you," Jenny said.

"Marley?" I asked. "How about the rest of you?"

"Of course we miss you, dingo," she said. "But I mean Marley really, *really* misses you. He's driving us all bonkers."

The night before, Marley had paced and sniffed the entire house over and over, looking for me. He poked through every room, looking behind doors and in closets. He struggled to get upstairs. When he couldn't find me there, he came back down again and began his search all over again.

"He was really out of sorts," Jenny said.

Marley even braved the steep, slippery wooden basement steps. Once down there, he could not get back up again. He stood yipping and whining until Jenny and the kids came to his rescue, holding him beneath the shoulders and hips and boosting him up step by step.

At bedtime, instead of sleeping beside our bed as he normally did, Marley camped out on the landing at the top of the stairs. That way he'd know if I came out of hiding or arrived home during the night—just in case I had snuck out without telling him. He wasn't taking any chances.

That's where Marley was the next morning when Jenny went downstairs to make breakfast. A couple hours passed before it dawned on her that he still had not shown his face, which was highly unusual. He was almost always the first one down the steps each morning, charging ahead of us and banging his tail against the front door to go out. She found him sleeping soundly on the floor tight against my side of the bed. Then she saw why. When she had gotten up, she had pushed her pillows over to my side of the bed. Beneath the covers, they formed a large lump where I usually slept. With his Mr. Magoo eyesight, Marley mistook the pile of feathers for his master.

"He absolutely thought you were in there," Jenny said. "I could just tell he did. He was convinced you were sleeping in!" We laughed together on the phone, and then

Jenny said, "You've got to give him points for loyalty."

I did. Devotion had always come easily to our dog.

I had been back from my trip for only a week when the crisis we knew could come at any time arrived. I was in the bedroom getting dressed for work when I heard a big crash. Conor screamed, "Help! Marley fell down the stairs!" I came running and found Marley in a heap at the bottom of the long staircase, struggling to get to his feet.

Jenny and I raced to him and ran our hands over his body, gently squeezing his limbs, pressing his ribs, massaging his spine. Nothing seemed to be broken. With a groan, Marley made it to his feet, shook off, and walked away without even limping. Conor had witnessed the fall. He said Marley had started down the stairs, but after just two steps realized everyone was still upstairs. So he attempted an about-face. As he tried to turn around, his hips dropped out from beneath him. He tumbled in a freefall down the entire length of the stairs.

"Wow, was he lucky!" I said. "A fall like that could have killed him."

"I can't believe he didn't get hurt," Jenny said. "He's like a cat with nine lives."

But Marley had gotten hurt. Within minutes he was stiffening up, and by the time I arrived home from work that night, Marley couldn't move. He seemed to be sore everywhere. He couldn't put any weight at all on his front left leg. I could squeeze it without him yelping, and I suspected he had pulled a tendon. When he saw me, he tried to struggle to his feet to greet me. It was no use. His left front paw was useless. With his weak back legs, he just had no power to do anything. Marley was down to one good limb. He finally made it up and tried to hop on three paws to get to me. His back legs caved in, and he collapsed back to the floor. Jenny gave him an aspirin and held a bag of ice to his front leg. Eternally playful Marley kept trying to eat the ice cubes.

By 10:30 that night, he was no better. He hadn't been out to pee since one that afternoon. He had been holding his urine for nearly ten hours. I had no idea how to get him outside and back in again so he could relieve himself. Straddling him and clasping my hands beneath his chest, I lifted him to his feet. Together we waddled our way to the front door. I held him up as he hopped along.

But out on the porch stoop Marley froze. A steady rain was falling, and the steps were slick and wet. He didn't know what to do.

"Come on," I said. "Just a quick pee and we'll go right back inside." He would have no part of it. I wished

I could have persuaded him to just pee right on the porch and be done with it. But I couldn't teach this old dog that new trick.

Marley hopped back inside and stared up at me. He seemed to be apologizing for what he knew was coming. "We'll try again later," I said. Just then he half-squatted on his three remaining legs and emptied his full bladder on the foyer floor. A puddle spread out around him. It was the first time since he was a tiny puppy that Marley had peed in the house.

The next morning Marley was better, though still hobbling about like an invalid. We got him outside, where he peed and pooped without problem. On the count of three, Jenny and I lifted him up the porch stairs to get him back inside.

"I have a feeling that Marley will never go upstairs in this house again," I told her. It was obvious he had climbed his last staircase. From now on, he would have to get used to living and sleeping on the ground floor.

Later that day, I was upstairs working on my computer in the bedroom when I heard a commotion on the stairs. I stopped typing and listened. It was a famil-iar sound—like a horse was galloping up a gangplank. I looked at the bedroom doorway and held my breath. A few seconds later, Marley popped his head around the corner and came into the room. His eyes brightened when he spotted me. "So there you are!" they said.

"Marley, you made it!" I exclaimed. "You old hound! I can't believe you're up here!" He smashed his head into my lap, begging for an ear rub, which I figured he had earned.

Later, as I sat on the floor with him and scruffed his neck, he twisted his head around and gamely gummed my wrist in his jaws. It was a sign of the playful puppy still in him. The night before, I had prepared myself for the worst—Marley's death. Today he was panting and pawing and trying to slime my hands off. Just when I thought his long, lucky run was over, he was back.

I pulled his head up and made him look me in the eyes. "You're going to tell me when it's time, right?" I said. It was really more of a statement than a question. I didn't want to have to make the decision on my own. "You'll let me know, won't you?"

22

The Big Meadow

Winter arrived early that year. As the days grew short and the winds howled through the frozen branches, we huddled together in our snug home. I chopped and split a winter's worth of firewood and stacked it by the back door. Jenny made hearty soups and homemade breads, and the children once again sat in the window and waited for the snow to arrive.

I awaited the first snowfall, too, but with a quiet sense of dread. I wondered how Marley could possibly make it through another tough winter. The previous one had been hard enough on him. Since then he'd gotten even weaker. I wasn't sure how he would be able to navigate ice-glazed sidewalks, slippery stairs, and a snow-covered yard.

On a blustery Sunday night in mid-December, Jenny declared a family movie night. The kids raced to pick out a video, and I whistled for Marley. Together we went outside to fetch a basket of maple logs off the woodpile. He poked around in the frozen grass as I loaded up the wood, standing with his face into the wind and his wet nose sniffing the icy air. I clapped my hands and waved my arms to get his attention. He followed me inside, hesitating at the front porch steps before gathering up his courage and lurching forward, dragging his back legs up behind him.

Inside, I got the fire humming as the kids popped the movie in the VCR. The flames leaped and the heat filled the room. As usual, Marley claimed the best spot for himself, directly in front of the hearth. I lay down on the floor a few feet from him and propped my head on a pillow, watching the fire more than the movie. Marley didn't want to lose his warm spot, but he couldn't miss his chance. His favorite human was at ground level lying flat on his back, utterly defenseless. Who was the alpha male now? His tail began pounding the floor. Then he started wiggling his way in my direction. He sashayed from side to side on his belly, his rear legs stretched out behind him. Soon he was pressed up against me, grinding his head into my ribs. The minute I reached out to pet him, it was all over. He pushed himself up on his paws, and shook hard, showering me in loose fur. He stared down at me, his billowing jowls hanging right over my face. When I started to laugh, he took this as a green light to advance. Before I quite knew what was happening, he had straddled my chest with his front paws and, in one big freefall, collapsed on top of me in a heap.

"Ugh!" I screamed under his weight. "Full-frontal Lab attack!" The kids squealed with laughter. Marley could not believe his good fortune. I wasn't even trying to get him off me. He squirmed. He drooled. He licked me all over the face and nuzzled my neck. I could barely breathe under his weight. After a few minutes I slid him half off me, where he remained through most of the movie. His head, shoulder, and one paw rested on my chest and the rest of him pressed against my side.

I didn't say so to anyone in the room, but I found

myself clinging to the moment, knowing there would not be too many more like it. Marley was in the quiet dusk of a long and eventful life. Looking back on it later, I would recognize that night in front of the fire for what it was, our farewell party. I stroked his head until he fell asleep. Then I stroked it some more.

Four days later, we packed the minivan. Our family was headed to Disney World. It would be the children's first Christmas away from home, and they were wild with excitement. Jenny delivered Marley to the veterinarian's office. She had arranged for him to spend our week away in the intensive care unit, where the doctors and workers could keep their eyes on him around the clock and he would not be riled by the other dogs.

It was a great family vacation. On the long drive back north we went over the pros and cons of each ride, each meal, each swim, each moment. When we were halfway through Maryland, just four hours from home, my cell phone rang. It was one of the workers from the vet's office. Marley was acting lethargic, she said, and his hips had begun to droop worse than normal. He seemed to be in discomfort. She said the vet wanted our permission to give him a shot and pain medication.

"Sure," I said. "Keep him comfortable, and we'll be there to pick him up tomorrow."

Jenny arrived to bring him home the following afternoon, December 29. Marley looked tired and a little out of sorts, but not ill. As we had been warned, his hips were weaker than ever. A worker helped Jenny lift him into the minivan. But within a half hour of getting him home, he was retching. Clear, thick mucus coated his throat, and he was trying to clear it. Jenny let him out in the front yard, and he simply lay on the frozen ground. He could not or would not budge.

Jenny called me at work in a panic. "I can't get him back inside," she said. "He's lying out there in the cold and he won't get up." I left immediately. By the time I got home forty-five minutes later, she had managed to get him to his feet and back in the house. I found him sprawled on the dining-room floor, clearly distressed and clearly not himself.

For thirteen years, it had always been the same. I'd walk into the house. He'd jump to his feet, stretching, shaking, panting, and banging his tail into everything. Not on this day. His eyes followed me as I walked into the room, but he did not move his head. I knelt beside him and rubbed his snout. No reaction. He did not try to gum my wrist. He did not want to play. He did not even lift his head. His eyes were far away, and his tail lay limp on the floor.

After several minutes, Marley slowly stood up on shaky legs and tried to retch again, but nothing would come out. That's when I noticed his stomach. It looked bigger than usual, and it was hard to the touch. My heart sank. I knew what this meant. I called the veterinarian's office and described Marley's bloated stomach.

"The doctor says to bring him right in," the receptionist told me.

Jenny and I did not have to say a word to each other. We both understood that the moment had arrived. We prepared the kids, telling them Marley had to go to the hospital. We explained that the doctors were going to try to make him better, but that he was very sick.

As I was getting ready to go, I looked at Jenny and the kids. They were huddled around Marley saying their good-byes. They each got to pet him and have a few last moments with him. Still, the kids remained positive that Marley would soon be back, good as new. After all, he'd been there with them their whole lives. He had to return.

"Get all better, Marley," Colleen said in her little voice.

With Jenny's help, I got him into the back of my car. She gave him a last quick hug, and I drove off with him, promising to call as soon as I learned something. He lay on the floor in the backseat with his head resting on the center hump. I drove with one hand on the wheel and the other stretched behind me so I could stroke his head and shoulders.

"Oh, Marley," I just kept saying.

In the parking lot of the animal hospital, I helped him out of the car. He stopped to sniff a tree where the other dogs all pee. Good old Marley was never too sick to be curious. I gave him a minute. Marley loved being outside, and I knew this might be the last time he'd have the chance. Then I tugged gently at his choke chain and led him into the lobby. Just inside the front door, he decided he had gone far enough and gingerly let himself down on the tile floor. When the vet's helpers and I were unable to get him back to his feet, they brought out a stretcher and slid him onto it. Then they disappeared with him behind the counter into the examining area.

A few minutes later, the vet came out and led me into an exam room, where she put a pair of X-ray films up on a light board. She showed me how his stomach had swollen to twice its normal size and how the intestines had twisted.

"It's a long shot, but I'm going to try to get his stomach back into place," she explained. It was exactly the same one-percent gamble Dr. Hopkinson had given over the summer.

"Okay," I said. "Please give it your best shot." It had worked once. It could work again. I silently hoped everything would be all right.

A half hour later, the vet emerged with a grim face. She had tried three times and was unable to open the blockage. "At this point, our only real option is to go into surgery," she said, then paused. "Or the most humane thing might be to put him to sleep."

Jenny and I had been through this decision five months earlier and had already made the hard choice. We did not want Marley to suffer anymore. He deserved better than that. We knew the right thing to do. Yet now, I stood frozen.

I told the doctor I wanted to step outside to call my wife. On the cell phone in the parking lot, I told Jenny that they had tried everything, but nothing had worked. We sat silently on the phone for a long moment before she said, "I love you, John."

"I love you, too, Jenny," I said.

I walked back inside and asked the doctor if I could have a couple minutes alone with him.

"Take all the time you need," she said.

I found him unconscious on the stretcher on the floor. I got down on my knees and ran my fingers through his fur, the way he liked. I ran my hand down his back. I lifted each floppy ear in my hands. I pulled up his lip and looked at his lousy, worn-out teeth. I picked up a front paw and cupped it in my hand. Then I dropped my forehead against his and sat there for a long time, as if I could send a message through our two skulls, from my brain to his. I wanted to make him understand some things.

"You know all that stuff we've always said about you?" I whispered. "What a total pain you are? Don't believe it. Don't believe it for a minute, Marley." He needed to know that, and something more, too. There was something I had never told him, that no one ever had. I wanted him to hear it before he went.

"Marley," I said. "You are a *great* dog."

I found the doctor waiting at the front counter. "I'm ready," I said. My voice was cracking. That surprised me because I had really believed I had been ready for this moment for months. I knew if I said another word I would break down and cry, so I just nodded. She led me back to Marley, and I knelt beside him as she prepared the shot. I cradled his head in my hands.

"Are you okay?" she asked. I nodded yes.

The vet gave him the shot, then listened to his heart. It had slowed way down but not stopped. He was a big dog. She gave him a second shot. A minute later, she listened again and said, "He's gone." She left me alone with him, and I gently lifted one of his eyelids. The doctor was right. Marley was gone.

I walked out to the front desk and paid the bill. A few minutes later, she and an assistant wheeled out a cart with a large black bag on it and helped me lift it into the back seat. The doctor shook my hand.

"I'm so sorry," she said. "I did my best."

"It was his time," I said, then thanked her and drove away.

In the car on the way home, I started to cry. It only lasted a few minutes. By the time I pulled into the driveway, I was dry-eyed again. I left Marley in the car and went inside where Jenny was sitting up, waiting. The children were all in bed asleep. We would tell them in the morning. We fell into each other's arms and both started weeping. I tried to describe it to her, to assure her he was already deeply asleep when the end came, that there was no panic, no pain. But I couldn't find the words. So we simply rocked each other in our arms. Later, we went outside and together lifted the heavy black bag out of the car and into the garden cart, which I rolled into the garage for the night.

23

Beneath the Cherry Trees

I had trouble sleeping that night. An hour before dawn I slid out of bed and dressed quietly, careful not to wake Jenny. In the kitchen, I drank a glass of water and stepped out into a light, slushy drizzle. I grabbed a shovel and pickax and walked to the white pines that Marley had made his personal potty the winter before. I had decided to bury him in the pea patch beside the pines.

The temperature was in the mid thirties, so the ground wasn't frozen. In the half-dark, I began to dig.

Once I was through a thin layer of topsoil, I hit heavy, dense clay studded with rocks. The digging was slow and hard. After fifteen minutes, I peeled off my coat and paused to catch my breath. After thirty minutes, I was in a sweat. I hadn't even dug down two feet yet. After forty-five minutes, I struck water. The hole began to fill. And fill. Soon a foot of muddy cold water covered the bottom. I fetched a bucket and tried to bail it, but more water just seeped in. There was no way I could possibly lay Marley down in that icy swamp. No way.

My heart was pounding as if I had just run a marathon. Despite the work I had invested in it, I abandoned the hole. I scouted the yard, stopping where the lawn met the woods at the bottom of the hill. Two big native cherry trees arched above me. These were the same trees Marley and I had narrowly missed on our wild toboggan ride.

"This feels right," I said, and sank my shovel in the ground between them. The soil was soft, and digging went easily. Soon I had an oval hole four feet deep. When the hole was done, I went inside and found all three kids up, sniffling quietly. Jenny had just told them.

I told them it was okay to cry and that owning a dog always ended with this sadness because dogs just don't live as long as people do. I told them how Marley was sleeping when they gave him the shot and that he didn't feel a thing. He just drifted off and was gone.

"I didn't get to say a real good-bye to him," Colleen said. She thought he would be coming home.

"I said good-bye for all of us," I told her.

Conor showed me something he had made to go in the grave with Marley. It was a drawing of a big red heart. Under the heart, he had written, "To Marley, I hope you know how much I loved you all of my life. You were always there when I needed you. Through life or death, I will always love you. Your brother, Conor Richard Grogan."

Colleen drew a picture of a girl with a big yellow dog and beneath it, with spelling help from her brother, she wrote, "P.S. – I will never forget you."

I went out alone and wheeled Marley's body down the hill. I laid an armful of soft pine boughs on the floor of the hole. Then I lifted the heavy body bag off the cart and down into the hole as gently as I could. I opened the bag to see him one last time and positioned him in a comfortable, natural way—just as he might be lying in front of the fireplace, curled up, head tucked around to his side.

"Okay, Big Guy, this is it," I said. I closed up the bag and returned to the house to get Jenny and the kids.

As a family, we walked down to the grave. Conor and Colleen had sealed their notes back-to-back in a plastic bag. I placed it right beside Marley's head. Patrick used his jackknife to cut five pine boughs, one for each of us. And one by one, we dropped them in the hole, their scent rising around us. We paused for a moment.

"Marley, we love you," we said all together as if we had rehearsed it.

I picked up the shovel and tossed the first scoop of dirt in.

When the hole was half filled, I took a break and we all walked up to the house, where we sat around the kitchen table and told funny Marley stories. One minute we were crying. The next we were laughing. Jenny told the story of Marley going bonkers during the filming of *The Last Home Run* when a stranger picked up Baby Conor. I told about all the leashes he had chewed and the time he peed on our neighbor's ankle. We described all the things he had destroyed and the thousands of dollars he had cost us. We could laugh about it now.

"Marley's spirit is up in dog heaven now," I told the kids. "He's in a giant golden meadow, running free. And his hips are good again. And his hearing is back, and his eyesight is sharp, and he has all his teeth. He's back in his prime—chasing rabbits all day long."

"And having endless screen doors to crash through," Jenny added. The image of him barging his way oafishly through heaven made everyone laugh.

In the days immediately after we buried Marley, the whole family went silent. For years we'd loved telling funny Marley stories. Now we couldn't talk about him. It was just too painful.

Colleen had the most trouble. She could not bear to hear his name or see his photo. Tears would well in her eyes and she would clench her fists and say angrily, "I don't want to talk about him!"

Every night for thirteen years, Marley was waiting for me at the door when I came home from work. Walking in now at the end of the day was the most painful part of all. The house seemed silent and empty. It was not quite home anymore. Jenny vacuumed like a fiend, try-ing to get up the bucketfuls of Marley fur that had been falling out in giant clumps for the past couple years. Slowly the signs of the old dog disappeared. One morning I went to put on my shoes, and inside them I found a layer of Marley fur. It had been picked up by my socks from walking on the floors and gradually deposited inside the shoes. I just sat and looked at it. I actually stroked it with two fingers and smiled. I held it up to show Jenny. "We're not getting rid of him that easy," I said.

She laughed, but that evening she blurted out, "I miss him. I mean I really, *really* miss him. I ache-inside miss him."

"I know," I said. "I do, too."

I wanted to write a farewell column to Marley in the *Philadelphia Inquirer*, but I was afraid I would get too mushy. I knew I wanted to be honest. Marley was a funny, bigger-than-life bad boy who never did learn to obey very well. Honestly, he just might have been the world's worst-behaved dog. But he knew from the start what it meant to be man's best friend.

That weekend I took a long walk through the woods, and by the time I arrived at my newspaper office on Monday, I knew what I wanted to say about the dog that touched my life, the one I would never forget.

I began the column by describing my walk down the

hill with the shovel at dawn and how odd it was to be outdoors without Marley at my side. "And now here I was alone," I wrote, "digging him this hole."

I gave a lot of thought to how I should describe him, and this is what I settled on: "No one ever called him a great dog—or even a good dog. He was as wild as a banshee and as strong as a bull. He crashed joyously through life with a gusto most often associated with natural disasters. As for brains, let me just say he chased his tail till the day he died, apparently convinced he was on the verge of a major canine breakthrough." But there was more to him than that. I also described his loyalty, gentleness, and his pure heart.

What I really wanted to say was how this animal had touched our souls and taught us some of the biggest lessons of our lives. "A person can learn a lot from a dog, even a loopy one like ours," I wrote. Marley taught me about living each day to the fullest. He taught me to seize the moment and follow my heart. He taught me to appreciate the simple things like a walk in the woods or a fresh snowfall. Mostly, he taught me how to be a good, loyal friend.

Was it possible for a dog—any dog, but especially a nutty, wild one like ours—to point humans to the things that really mattered in life? Things like loyalty, courage, and devotion. And the things that did not matter, too? A dog has no use for fancy cars or big homes or designer clothes. A waterlogged stick will do just fine. A dog judges others not by how they look but by who they are inside. A dog doesn't care if you are rich or poor, smart or dull. Give him your heart, and he will give you his. It was really quite simple.

As I wrote that farewell column to Marley, I realized it was all right there in front of us if we only opened our eyes. Sometimes it took a dog with stinky breath and bad manners to help us see what really counts in life. Despite all his flaws, Marley had given us a gift that no amount of money could buy. He gave us the gift of total, complete love. He taught us how to give it and how to accept it. When you have love, most of the other pieces fall into place.

I turned in my column and drove home for the night, feeling somehow lighter. It was as though a weight I did not even know I had been carrying was lifted from me.

24

Lucky

The days turned into weeks and winter melted into spring. Daffodils pushed up through the earth and bloomed around Marley's grave. Delicate white cherry blossoms floated down to rest on it. Gradually, life without our dog became more comfortable.

The summer after his death, we put a swimming pool in our yard. I could not help thinking how much Marley, our tireless water dog, would have loved it. In fact, he would have loved it more than any of us possibly could.

Without a dog shedding and drooling and tracking in dirt, the house was a lot easier to keep clean. And I loved walking barefoot in the grass without watching for piles of poop. The garden was definitely better off without a big, heavy-pawed rabbit chaser crashing through it. No doubt about it, life without a dog was easier and much simpler. We could take a weekend trip without arranging boarding. We could go out to dinner without worrying what family heirloom might be destroyed. The kids could eat without having to guard their plates. The trash can did not have to go up on the kitchen counter when we left. Now we could sit back and really enjoy a good lightning storm. I especially liked the freedom of moving around the house without a giant yellow magnet glued to my heels.

Still, as a family, we were not quite whole.

One morning in late summer I came down for breakfast, and Jenny handed me a section of the newspaper folded over to show an inside page.

"You're not going to believe this," she said.

Once a week, our local paper featured a dog from a rescue shelter that needed a home. The profile always featured a photograph of the dog, its name, and a brief description.

Staring up at me from the page was a face I instantly recognized. Our Marley. Or at least a dog that could have been his identical twin. He was a big male yellow Lab with an anvil head, furrowed brow, and floppy ears cocked back at a comical angle. He stared directly into the camera lens with a quivering intensity that made you just know that seconds after the picture was snapped he had knocked the photographer to the ground and tried to swallow the camera. Beneath the photo was the name—Lucky.

I read his sales pitch aloud. This is what Lucky had to say about himself: "Full of zip! I would do well in a home that is quiet while I am learning how to control my energy level. I have not had an easy life, so my new family will need to be patient with me and continue to teach me my doggie manners."

"My gosh," I exclaimed. "It's him. He's back from the dead."

"Reincarnation," Jenny said.

It was amazing how much Lucky looked like Marley and how much the description fit him, too. Full of zip? Problem controlling energy? Working on doggie manners? Patience required? We knew all about these phrases. They were positive ways of talking about problem pooches. We had used them ourselves.

And from the description, we knew our crazy dog was back—young and strong again, and wilder than ever. We both stood there, staring at the newspaper, not saying anything.

"I guess we could go look at him," I finally said.

"Just for the fun of it," Jenny added.

"Right. Just out of curiosity."

"What's the harm of looking?"

"No harm at all," I agreed.

"Well then," she said, "why not?"

"What do we have to lose?"